LOVERS' LEGENDS

Lovers' Legends
The Gay Greek Myths

Restored and retold by

Andrew Calimach

HAIDUK PRESS

Haiduk Press, LLC.
PO Box 1783
New Rochelle, NY
USA 10802-1783

www.haidukpress.com

Printed in the United States of America
This edition is printed on acid-free paper with recycled content.

Library of Congress Control Number: 2001119267

Publisher's Cataloging-in-Publication Data
(Provided by Quality Books, Inc.)

Calimach, Andrew
      Lovers' legends : the gay Greek myths / Andrew
Calimach — 1st ed.
      p. cm.
      Includes bibliographical references and index.
      ISBN 0-9714686-0-5
      1. Homosexuality—Mythology. 2. Mythology, Greek.
I. Title.
BL795.H6C35 2001   292'.178257662
                                 QBI01-701 196

British Library Cataloguing in Publication Data
A catalogue record for this book is available from the British Library.

To Allen Ginsberg,

dharma brother and

heart father.

OLD LOVE STORY

Some think the love of boys is wicked in the world, forlorn
Character corrupting, worthy mankind's scorn
Or eyes that weep and breasts that ache for lovely youth
Have no mouth to speak for mankind's general truth
Nor hands to work manhood's fullest delight
Nor hearts to make old women smile day and night
Nor arms to warm young girls to dream of love
Nor thighs to satisfy thighs, nor breath men can approve —
Yet think back to the time our epic world was new
When Gilgamesh followed the shade of his friend Enkidu
Into Limbo's dust to talk love man to man
So younger David enamored of young Jonathan
Wrote songs that women and men still chant for calm
Century after century under evergreen or palm
A love writ so sacred on our bible leaf
That heart fire warms cold millennial grief.
Same time Akilleos won the war at Troy
Grieving Patroklos' body, his dead warrior boy
(One nation won the world by reading Greek for this
And fell when Wilde was gaoled for his Bellboy's kiss)
Marvelous Zeus himself took lightning eagle shape
Down-cheeked Ganymede enjoyed God's thick-winged rape
And lived a youth forever, forever as can be,
Serving his nectar to the bearded deity
The whole world knew the story, the whole world laughed in awe
That such love could be the Thunder of immortal Law.
When Socrates climbed his ladder of love's degrees
He put his foot in silence on rough Alcibiades
Wise men still read Plato, whoever they are,
Plato whose love-lad Aster was his morning star
Plato whose love-lad was in death his star of Night
Which Shelley once witnessed as eternal light.
Catullus and tough Horace were slaves to glad young men
Loved them, cursed them, always fell in love again
Caesar conquered the world, top Emperor Power
Lay soft on the breast of his soldier of the hour
Even Jesus Christ loved his young John most

Later he showed him the whole Heavenly Host
Old Rome approved a beautiful bodied youth
Antinous Hadrian worshiped with Imperial Truth
Told in the calm gaze of his hundred stone
Statues standing fig-leafed in the Vatican.
Michelangelo lifted his young hand to smooth
The belly of his Bacchus, a sixteen-year youth
Whose prick stands up he's drunk, his eyes gaze side-
Ways to his right hand held up shoulder high
Waving a cup of grape, smart kid, his nose is sharp,
His lips are new, slightly opened as if parted to take a sip of
    purple nakedness,
Taste Michelangelo's mortal-bearded kiss,
Or if a hair-hooved horny Satyr happens to pass
Fall to the ground on his strong little marble ass.
Michelangelo loved him! What young stud
Stood without trousers or shirt, maybe even did
What the creator wanted him to in bed
Lay still with the sculptor's hand cupped on his head
Feeling up his muscles, feeling down his bones
Palm down his back and thighs, touching his soft stones —
What kind of men were the Slaves he tied to his bed?
And who stood still for David naked foot to head?
But men love the muscles of David's abdomen
And come with their women to see him again and again.

Enough, I've stayed up all night with these boys
And all my life enjoyed their handsome joys
I came with many companions to this Dawn
Now I am tired and must set my pen down
Reader, Hearer, this time Understand
How kind it is for man to love a man,
Old love and Present, future love the same
Hear and Read what love is without shame.

I want people to understand! They can! They can! They can!
So open your ears and hear the voice of the classical Band.

Allen Ginsberg, October 26, 1981

CONTENTS

Charioteer and Quadriga

Beloved Charioteers

The Greek World

If you were to peer closely into an ancient Greek vase painting, vibrant with life and detail, you might just find yourself pulled beyond its surface, drawn into another world. At first you might feel quite at home. It is a land of paved streets lined with hot-food stands, public gyms, swimming pools, steam baths, democratic government, doctors, tailors, lawyers, cooks, teachers. You might book passage to Egypt to see the pyramids, and there you'd find guides to usher you around, and peddlers hawking trinkets. Every four years you could attend the Olympic games, and any educated person could tell you the world was round, and even its size.

Were you to look closer still, some less familiar features might take shape. This Greece is still pristine: virgin forests cover hills and mountain slopes where rocky scrubland spreads today, and lions, boar and deer roam at will in an unpolluted world. The human realm is rife with divisions: Freemen on one side, passing orders; slaves on the other, doing the work, a thin divide between the two, easily crossed if Fortune smiled or frowned. The women keep to one wing of the house, the men to another; *they* call the shots here. Before the doors of the well-to-do, herms stand at attention: carved stone totems, eyes gazing out at the passers-by, penises erect, to snag fertility and fortune. Here, a youth might well be ashamed *not* to have a lover, and people might wonder why men did not vie for his affection. Of course, male love, like all Greek life, was bounded by customs and regulations.

There was a right way to engage in such a relationship, and a right time as well. Strato of Sardis, the second century CE Lydian epigrammatist, perhaps said it best:

Leading a child astray before the time is ripe
Is a great error for his lover.
Yet, after you are grown, to still submit
To what is done with youths is twice as shameful.
But comes a time, Moirus, when it's no longer shameful
   and not yet,
And now is come that time for you and me.[1]

Myth itself points to what "that time" might have been: Iolaus is
said to have been sixteen when he accompanied Hercules on his labors.
This was also Narcissus' age at the peak of his beauty, according to
Ovid. Plato, too, held in highest esteem those lovers who "...fall in
love with boys old enough to think for themselves – in other words,
with boys who are nearly grown up."[2]

Some think that in prehistoric Greece male love was an integral part
of initiation rites.[3] By classical times, however, adult *lovers* were pursuing

Courtship ritual [4]

teenaged *beloveds*.[5] Greek ideals endowed these affairs with clear pedagogic functions: Male love was held to be an apprenticeship for manhood, a way to learn about warriorship, culture, and proper behavior. The relationship was defined by mutual obligations. For instance, the youth typically served as his lover's charioteer,[6] driving the horses in battle while the older man wielded the weapons. On the other hand, the lover was held responsible for the beloved's behavior – if the younger misbehaved, the elder of the pair was the one punished. The lover also saw to his beloved's education in philosophy and the arts.[7] As the poet Callimachus wrote in the third century BCE:

> You who upon youths cast longing eyes,
> The sage of Erchius[8] bids you be lovers of boys.
> Make love then to the young, the city with upstanding
>   men to fill.[9]

Of course, distinctions were made between what should be done with the sons of citizens and what could be done to slaves. Behind a facade of idealized male love, the sons of conquered foes were routinely enslaved and put to work in all-male brothels, as often as not after being castrated (with untold loss of life), in order to prolong their attractive years. Phaedo, the handsome Elian youth who lent his name to Plato's renowned dialogue, was bought (and freed) at Socrates' behest from just such an establishment. We would not be alone in reproaching some of our ancestors for their excesses: Their own contemporaries dragged them over the coals.[10]

On further inspection, other ironies unfold: Just as we may find some of the Greeks' practices objectionable, they would have thought as much of ours. Theirs was a warrior society in which the cult of masculinity led to the subjugation of women and sexual penetration of the vanquished. For all their adoration of the male form, they heaped contempt upon men who were perceived as effeminate or loved others their own age. This disapproval, however, is proof positive that, righteous fulminations aside, grown men loved each other even then. Indeed, it seems that if a couple carried on their love-making after the beloved matured, allowances were made: "The one who carried the calf can bear up the bull,"[11] the Greeks used to say, seemingly not without empathy.

The Myths

Exactly what were the gods and heroes? Fictions? Fairy tales? Far from it. To the Greeks,[12] they were the encounter with the divine, as well as true history; far more real to them than the ancient Greeks themselves are to us today. By means of myths, the Greeks stamped the names and the places they claimed as their own, their customs, their very existence, with the stamp of authenticity. Thus the myths remain an open window through which we can look upon our forefathers and the ways they imagined themselves.

The stories in this collection, restored from original sources in translation, outline the archetypal territory of Greek male love, as well as the boundaries crossed only at risk of divine retribution. We know of many more such tales, but they, as countless other treasures of ancient Greece, have been lost or destroyed. The list below, of gods and their lovers, suggests the breadth of the tradition, but is by no means complete.

- The champion of male love was Apollo, patron of culture and protector of the young. Besides Hyacinthus, Cyparissus, and Orpheus he had many beloveds whose stories have been lost.[13]
- The first god ever to love a man was Poseidon, who loved Pelops, and perhaps also Kaineus, to whom he granted invulnerability in exchange for his love.[14]
- The king of the gods, Zeus, was "set on fire" by the sight of Ganymede's thighs.[15]
- Hermes, as befits a protector god of the athletic fields, playgrounds of the handsome, had his beloved Antheus.
- Of Pan's boyfriends we know only one: Daphnis, whom he taught to play the panpipes.
- Dionysus loved Ampelos, "Vine,"[16] but of this god's affairs not much more is known, perhaps because they were part of his lost mysteries.[17]

In matters of male love, the heroes lived up to their title. The most prolific was Hercules, whose male lovers were, as the poet Theocritus assures us,[18] numberless. In the realm of passion Hercules was omnivorous, renowned for his prowess with women as well as with youths. His twelve labors are legend, but perhaps an even greater exploit was his encounter with the fifty daughters of

Zeus and Ganymede

Hercules, Eros and Iolaus

king Thespius. At the invitation of their father, he bedded them all in one night (except the youngest, who was too shy), and got them all with child, and all boys, of course. Of his many male beloveds,[19] we are told he loved wise Nestor best, even more than handsome Hylas or war-like Iolaus.[20] Many of the other heroes had minions as well,[21] and, though most of those accounts have been lost, we can still wonder at the abundance of such tales a Greek youth might have heard as he lounged in the shade of an ancient oak in the palestra, and at the way those myths might have colored his feelings and his thoughts.

Different Loves[1]

This 1700-year-old debate pits a lover of women against a lover of boys. The tale opens as Theomnestus, a young nobleman fond of boys and girls alike, asks his friend Lycinus which of the two he deems better.

Part I

LYCINUS: Since dawn, friend Theomnestus, you've filled my ears with love's games. I'd had it up to here with serious stuff, and thirsted for amusement. Man's spirit needs to take a break — it craves a bit of relaxation, a taste of pleasure. All morning long your vivid and delightful stories made me feel like Aristides the Milesian, that writer of steamy tales. I swear upon those loves of yours, to which you've presented such a broad target, I'm sorry indeed you've reached the end! I beg you, in the name of Aphrodite herself, should you think I am joking, tell me one more adventure with boys or girls; Come, search your memory! Besides, today is Hercules' festival — we need a sacrifice. I'm sure you know how wild this god is about Love; your tales will please him more than victims.

THEOMNESTUS: You'd sooner count the ocean's waves, or the rushing snowflakes, Lycinus, than all my loves. I think they've emptied out their quiver into me, so were they to go after another, their unarmed hand would only draw laughter. Ever since childhood gave way to youth, I yielded myself for them to feast upon me. Loves followed thick upon each other: before one ended, another began. They were like true Lernean[2] heads, more numerous than that of the Hydra, defying the flaming brands of Iolaus — as if fire could ever put out fire. No doubt there is a lodestone in my eyes that tirelessly draws all who are beautiful. I have even asked myself more than once whether so many favors were not some curse of Aphrodite. And yet I'm no child of Helios,[3] nor some insolent Lemnian,[4] nor that boor Hippolytus.[5]

Philosophers debating

LYCINUS: Spare me your hypocrisy, Theomnestus! What?! You would blame Fortune for a life awash in pretty women and boys in the flower of their youth? Perhaps we should hold atonement sacrifices to cure you of such a dread disease. All kidding aside, consider yourself lucky the gods did not fate you to the grimy toil of the farmer, the peregrinations of the merchant, or the dangers of army life. Your only care in the world is to stroll through wrestling schools reeking of massage oil, to primp the folds of your purple robe, or treat yourself to yet another fancy hairdo. Besides, these torments of love you gripe

Love gift

about only heap delight upon delight, and desire's bite is sweet. When you tempt, you joy in hope. When you win, you joy in pleasure: present and future hold only delight for you. Just now, as you were drawing up the tally of your loves with a precision worthy of Hesiod, your eyes melted, your voice flowed more sweetly than Lycambes' daughters',[6] and your whole demeanor shouted out you were in love with love, as well as with its memory. Come, if you've left out any scrap of your trek with Aphrodite, repair the fault right away: Hercules will have his victim whole.

THEOMNESTUS: This god, Lycinus, is an eater of oxen. What's more, he likes his victims steaming. If we should honor him with stories, mine have dragged on long enough and become stale. Your turn, please. Let your own Muse cast off her usual gravity and spend the day delighting together with the god! I see you do not favor one love over another, so please be an impartial judge: Tell me, who is better – the lover of boys, or one who delights in women? I, who am smitten by both, lean neither this way nor that, but keep in balance the two arms of the scale. You, who are untouched by either, give me your impartial opinion. Be frank, dear friend. Say which side you are on, now that I have told you of my loves. (Continued on page 37)

Tantalus
and the Olympians

When mortals first began to walk the earth, a great host descended upon the foothills of Sipylus, the holy mountain. At the command of Tantalus, their king, they raised a city there, the first ever built by man, and flung up massive walls around it, hewn to endure to the end of time. The Holder of the Earth had given Tantalus his own daughter, Dione, for wife, and she had already borne him two outstanding children. Pelops alone – their third child, a boy in the first bloom of youth – was unremarkable. The king and queen, however, only had eyes for him, and groomed him to follow his father on the throne.

The gods loved Tantalus intensely. Zeus himself counted the king among his closest friends. He opened wide the doors of Olympus to him, and often invited him to share the honor of the gods' table as no mortal before or since. Nor did Tantalus hold back: he filled his belly with nectar and ambrosia and won deathlessness for himself. The Olympians, who trusted the man completely, counseled with him over the workings of the world, and confided in

Zeus, king of Heaven

Poseidon

him their close-guarded mysteries. Little did they know
Tantalus betrayed their trust. Despite his love for them, he
stole their food from under their noses, handed it out to
his people, and revealed to them the secrets of the gods.

To thank the Olympians for all the meals he had
partaken of, Tantalus invited Zeus, and Poseidon, shaker of
the shining trident, and the other gods on high, to his well-
built halls for a splendid feast. Filled with devotion, he
pledged to put before them only the very best. On his way
home, however, he was beset by doubts, for he had no
inkling how to fulfill his promise. As he stepped through
the gates of the palace, his son Pelops ran up to greet him.
There and then the king realized he had nothing finer to

30

Pelops

offer the gods. Without a word to Dione, he secretly led
the boy away and slew him. He then hacked the body into
pieces, set all to boil in a pure three-legged cauldron, and
fixed a rich stew for his guests.

At the appointed hour the Olympians filed in and
ranged themselves around the banquet table. Tantalus
brought on the broken, boiled body of his son, served each   *40*
god a share. The cut of honor — the left shoulder — he laid
before Demeter, her, queen of mysteries. The indigo-robed
goddess reached out, allayed her hunger. But before the
other gods could tuck into their portions, Zeus'
compassion moved him to command the flesh and bones
be gathered up. He had them placed back in the cauldron,

then cast a spell upon it. Again they were set to boil, and old Fate went about joining the parts together. She came up short, however, for the shoulder was missing. Demeter, by way of thanking Tantalus for his offering, handed Fate one crafted of lustrous ivory, and light poured out of it, filling even the darkest corner of the hall. Fate fit the missing piece in place, lifted the body whole from the great cauldron, and then, by the will of the gods, the boy was given life again. •

Pelops moved out among the guests, and everyone's eyes were on him now: all his homeliness had boiled away, and his beauty glowed from every pore. Poseidon sat riveted, lost in wonder. The wild heart in him was tamed by desire, and he drank in the sight of the boy with the gleaming shoulder. The god chased after Pelops, lifted him into his chariot, and his golden horses flew up and away with them into the sky, to Zeus' palace in Olympus. Meanwhile, Dione, who had not been invited to the feast, was looking high and low for her son, but he had vanished. The queen was frantic. She sent men throughout Sipylus to bring back her child, but search as they might, they found no trace of him. In the end an envious neighbor drew her aside and whispered he had been boiled, and the gods had divvied up the morsels among themselves.

Dione's loss, however, was Poseidon's gain. He settled in with Pelops as lover and beloved, and fed his friend ambrosia to make him deathless. Often he took the boy riding in his gold chariot, and patiently taught him to bend the swift winged horses to his will. Pelops loved the great

50

60

70

bearded god, and hung on his every word. In no time at all
his skill as charioteer outshone that of any other man.
Poseidon kept the boy close. At feast times, Pelops was
always there by his side; filling the god's cup with nectar,
pouring for the guests as well. And his own father,   80
Tantalus, was one of the regulars. But he sipped only a
portion of his nectar – the rest he smuggled out.

Any man who thinks to fool the gods' eyes with his
doings makes a big mistake. Tantalus' thefts caught up with
him in the end, and the anger of Zeus deceived fell like a
thunderbolt upon the king and all his kin. The lord of
gods laid utter waste to Sipylus. He razed the city to the
ground and cast Tantalus into the deepest pit of Hades,
doomed him to eternal hunger and thirst. Zeus also made
Pelops pay for his father's crimes. He yanked him out of   90
Poseidon's arms, stripped him of immortality and chased
him from Olympus, sending him back to the fleeting
destiny of the human race.

The people of Sipylus, however, remembered their
beloved king when they rebuilt their
city. They raised up a great tomb
for Tantalus on the side of the
holy mountain, and often came to
pay him homage. And when
Pelops made it back from   100
Olympus, they seated him on the
throne and named him ruler in his
father's place.

Tantalus

Pelops in Pisa

In far-off Lydia, Pelops was ruler of the land. Though still a youth, his eyes had seen much already. He had rubbed shoulders with the Olympians, had been Poseidon's beloved, and the god had made him deathless — so deep was his love. Now, cast back among the mortals as he was, some of the magic and power of the gods still clung to him, some of their skills as well. Poseidon had taught him to drive a chariot as only a god might, and his words of advice still rang in Pelops' ears. Now that the first beard darkened his cheeks and his strength and build had reached full bloom, no one could best him at handling the nimble car, at driving the snorting, pawing team. But riding was the last thing on his mind. Pelops' thoughts had turned to marriage, and he dearly wished for a wife.

One day a Greek ship sailed in from far across the sea. It brought word of a contest and the rich prize that hung in the balance. Oinomaus, king of Pisa, was seeking a husband for his daughter, Hippodamia, a girl of rare beauty. To win her hand, the suitor had to defeat her father in a chariot race, or lose his life trying. When Pelops heard

Hippodamia and her mother

10

20

the news, he leaped at the chance. With the skills he had learned from Poseidon, success was in his grasp. He had a swift ship hauled out, rigged her well, set sail, and journeyed to Greece to win himself the girl.

Once in Pisa, he strode proudly up to Oinomaus' palace. But as he reached the gate, he saw a sight beyond belief: high on the wall above the entrance, the heads of twelve young men were spiked to the stone, some fresh and some just grinning skulls. They were Oinomaus' trophies, Pelops 30 learned, the heads of suitors who had come before, and their bodies had been rudely heaped together in an open pit. The spirits of the murdered men knew no rest, and their curses, uttered with dying words, hung over all who lived within that palace. Pelops trembled to see the gory sight and was sorry he had come. Just then, however,

40 Hippodamia happened by, noble of bearing, escorted by a bevy of handmaidens. Pelops glimpsed her face through her veil and was overcome by so much beauty. He pledged to free her from her fate, to purify her of the murders too, if the gods willed it. After all the butchery, Hippodamia was loath to look at another suitor, but the moment she set eyes on Pelops she was swept away by his loveliness, by the magic streaming from him, and by the lightning flashing from his eyes; she would have moved heaven and earth to have him for a husband.

Poseidon and Pelops

Hippodamia was desperate. It was past time for her to   50
wed, day and night she dreamt about it. Time and again she
begged her father for her freedom, crying hot tears. At first
the old king refused outright, but in the end he relented,
he offered her a bargain: He would give her in marriage to
anyone who asked. First, however, the man had to race him
to Poseidon's temple in Corinth. The suitor was to take up
Hippodamia in his chariot and gallop away. Oinomaus
would sacrifice a ram to Zeus and, afterward, give chase.
If the suitor won, the girl and the throne of Pisa were his.
But if the king ever caught up, the man's blood would slake   60
the thirsty earth, and that of his horses too. Oinomaus had

The flying chariot

no fear of losing. His black mares were by far the best in all of Greece and his charioteer, dear to his heart, was without peer. Myrtilus was his name, a son of Hermes, the trickster god. Myrtilus loved Hippodamia himself but was terrified to race, so he served the king instead.

Thus Oinomaus stood in the way of his daughter's marriage. He had his reasons: For one thing, a seer had warned he would meet his death at the hand of his son-in-law. For another, he had fallen in love with his own daughter, and wanted her for himself. Hippodamia's love for her father turned to loathing. Zeus saw it all, was sickened by the king's savage ways, and turned his face away from Oinomaus.

Love for Hippodamia drove Pelops on, but he feared
the cruelty of the king, and his confidence was broken.
Only the memory of the girl kept him from turning tail
and making for home. As night came on, he walked alone
to the shore of the gray sea, and called aloud to his old
lover. He straight away appeared out of the darkness, close
at hand. Pelops addressed the god with heartfelt words: *80*

Libation at Zeus' altar

O, Poseidon! If you had any joy of our love,
Aphrodite's sweet gift, stay the bronze spear of
Oinomaus, speed me on the swiftest of chariots
down by Pisa's river, and clothe me about in
strength, for he has already killed twelve, and
puts off his daughter's wedlock.

Racing for Corinth

Great danger does not take hold of a coward;
since we are all destined to die, why should one
sit to no purpose in darkness and find a
nameless old age, without any part of glory his
own? No, to me falls this hazard, to you to grant   *90*
me success!

The god of the thundering seas smiled, nodded. Then, in answer to Pelops' prayer, four winged horses rose from the deep, harnessed to a golden chariot that rolled over the waves without wetting its axles.

Back in Pisa, Pelops sealed his pact with Oinomaus with a libation at the altar of Zeus and readied for the contest, but every time his eyes fell on the bloody trophies spiked to that high wall, fresh doubt clawed his breast. He pulled aside the king's charioteer and spelled things out for him: "Listen, Myrtilus. I see from your glances the girl is dear to you, too. Help *me* win, and the first night with her is yours to enjoy, I swear it upon all that is sacred!" Myrtilus did

100

Oinomaus giving chase

26

not need to be asked twice. The night before the race, as
he mounted the chariot's wheels on their polished axles,
Myrtilus switched the bronze linchpins that held the
wheels in place with fake ones made of beeswax.

The day of the race dawned at last. Pelops stepped aboard
his golden chariot, lifted Hippodamia to his side, and cracked
the whiplash. The winged horses sprang at his urging, and in
the blink of an eye left Pisa far behind. Pelops rode for dear 110
life, one eye on the road ahead, another on the road behind,
in fear of the brutal king. Oinomaus took his time, offered
an unblemished ram to war-like Zeus, prayed for success.
Little did he know the god, sick of all the slaughter, now
turned a deaf ear to his plea. The king then climbed aboard
his waiting car, and bade his driver set off in hot pursuit.

They flew on like the wind, farther than ever before, but
Pelops was nowhere to be seen. In no time at all, sacred
Corinth itself hove into view, and the old king raged at the
thought the race was lost. Just then, before them on the 120
rocky path, gleamed Pelops' golden car. Oinomaus drew
back his arm to spear the upstart between the shoulders, to
rip out his life. But as he did, the chariot hit a bump, both
wheels flew off their axles, and the car overturned and
broke into pieces. Myrtilus rolled with the fall, but the old
king pitched forward into the dust, tangled in the reins.
The horses galloped on, dragging Oinomaus over the sharp
rocks, and with his last breath the old king cursed Myrtilus
for his betrayal. As for the gory palace of Oinomaus, Zeus
lord of lightning struck it with his thunderbolt, wrapped 130
it in tongues of flame, burned it to the ground.

Pelops pressed on, in no time rolled up to Poseidon's
temple, and offered there a white-hot prayer of thanks to
his old lover. Hippodamia was his now, as was the throne
of Pisa. He then mounted the golden car and headed, by
way of the sea, for his new home, his bride and Myrtilus
flanking him. The new king, however, was not about to
lend his wife out to anyone. As soon as they left land
behind, he gave Myrtilus a mighty kick, hurling him from
140   the chariot to the bottom of the sea, drowning him in its
wine-dark waters. As he slipped beneath the waves,
Myrtilus laid a heavy curse upon Pelops and his house for
this treachery. Hermes set his son, the charioteer, among
the stars, and saw to it that his curse loomed unwavering
over the house of Pelops. Disaster rolled relentless over the
land of Pisa, despite the temple to Myrtilus that Pelops
raised in atonement, hoping to appease that angry ghost
with sacrifices over an empty tomb. Hippodamia gave her
husband many children over the years, but horror after
150   horror befell their family, for Hermes struck such discord
between the sons that they shattered the law of
brotherhood, and paid for blood with blood.

Pelops and Myrtilus

Goldenhorse breaking a stallion

Laius and
Goldenhorse

After many a day on the road, a weary band of
travelers struggled to the gates of King Pelops'
palace in Pisa and hailed the guard: "Open up!
Laius, prince of Thebes has come," their chief called out.
The heavy gates swung open and the men stumbled in, a
few battle-hardened warriors and one gangling youth.
When they had rested, their chief spun his tale: Usurpers
had grabbed the reins of power in Thebes, killed all who
stood in their way. Laius, the dead king's son, didn't stand
a chance. A few loyal subjects had fled with the boy in
dark of night, had saved his life. He needed a protector
now, Pelops was their best hope. Would the king grant
the prince safe harbor?

Pelops welcomed Laius as one of his own, and made
room for him at table next to his sons. The twins, Atreus
and Thyestes, he had fathered with his faithful wife,
Hippodamia. Handsome little Goldenhorse, however, he
had fathered on the sly with a nymph. Pelops kept him
close, even though Hippodamia could not stand the sight
of the curly blond imp.

10

20

Laius and the twins were of an age. They spent all day together – no one could part them. They outdid each other in hunting and war games, steeled their bodies in the wrestling school. The years flew by and Laius ripened into manhood in Pelops' house, praying someday to repay the king's hospitality. The twins likewise blossomed into men like gods, and Hippodamia swelled with pride to see their strength. She spared no effort in grooming them for power, for someday the kingdom would be theirs.

30   That was the last thing Pelops wanted. He loved Goldenhorse the best of all his sons, and meant to set *him* on the throne. To carry out his plans, however, he needed a man he could trust completely. He summoned Laius, and let him in on his designs: his son had to be taught the skills of princes, for he had much to learn before he could rule. Pelops charged Laius to tutor Goldenhorse, to teach him the charioteer's art. Laius saw no way out, he was bound to repay the king's welcome. He bowed low, thanked Pelops for the honor, and pledged to fulfill his

40   wishes to the letter.

From that day on, each rose-red fingered dawn found Laius and the boy already hard at work, riding the polished bentwood chariot, putting the rapid horses through their paces. Goldenhorse drank it all in. The Nemean games were drawing near and his heart pounded with thoughts of glory, racing other Greek princes, even winning a champion's laurels, if so the gods chose. But as Laius cooly taught Goldenhorse to turn the spirited horses to his will, his heart flamed with desire for the boy. In a thousand

different ways he tried to win his love, but nothing worked. *50*
Goldenhorse kept aloof.

The kidnapping

The games were about to start, so Laius and his pupil
set out from Pisa, with Pelops' blessings, for the green
valleys of Nemea. To spare the boy's strength for the races,
Laius took the reins. But when they reached the famous city
he did not halt, he picked up the pace instead. Goldenhorse
pleaded, begged, and threatened, but Laius just flogged the
team on, breakneck on. He stopped his ears to the boy's
cries and never curbed the horses' headlong career until the
towers of Thebes loomed overhead. There Laius claimed *60*
the throne as his birthright, and strong-armed Goldenhorse
to live with him as his beloved. "I know what I am doing,
but nature forces me," he told the boy. The Thebans were

overjoyed at the return of their rightful king, and
kept their counsel about the unlawful
doings at the royal palace.

As soon as Pelops learned Laius
had kidnapped his son, he called his
men to arms and marched on Thebes.
70   Nor did Hippodamia waste any time.
She summoned Atreus and Thyestes:
without a word to Pelops, they
leaped aboard a chariot and raced
away, hell-bent
for Laius' palace.
Goldenhorse thrilled to see
his brothers, so grateful to be
delivered from his life of
shame. But as the three of
80   them walked out the palace
gates, the twins grabbed hold
of the boy and pitched him
head-first into a well, drowning
him in its dark waters.

Meanwhile, Pelops' army sped
like the wind and soon was arrayed
many deep before the walls of Thebes.
The king's emissary galloped into the
city, only to discover that Goldenhorse
90   was dead. Pelops shook with rage and
grief. "Never again shall these two
sons of mine set foot upon the soil

Hippodamia

of my country," he commanded. And he was furious with
his wife. Hippodamia trembled before her husband's wrath.
She fled with her sons into exile and hung herself.

When king Pelops came to Laius, however, he
remembered the love god's power to turn the heads of men,
and spared his life. But the king laid upon Laius a father's
curse, and called down the anger of the gods upon the
royal house of Thebes. Disaster dogged the Thebans and   *100*
horrors without end befell Laius and his kin: his own son
murdered him, then fouled his own mother's bed, sowing
his seed where himself had been sown – doomed Oedipus.

Aphrodite

Different Loves

In answer to Theomenstus' request, Lycinus recounts an argument he had recently refereed between two friends, whose tastes in love were opposed. The three of them were about to embark upon a journey, but first a debate comparing male and female love was held, to put an end to the annoying bickering between Lycinus' friends on the subject of love. Lycinus' recollections find him and his two friends holed up in a shady grove by Aphrodite's temple. Charicles is a young Corinthian bon-vivant, mad about women, and Callicratidas, an important Athenian politician, with a bottomless thirst for youths. The debate is about to start.[1]

Part II

LYCINUS: Charicles passed his hand over his brow and, after a moment of silence, began thus:

CHARICLES: I call upon you, my Lady Aphrodite, uphold my plea for this, your cause! Every task, regardless how small, attains perfection if you but grant it the least measure of your mercy; but matters of love have special need of you, for you are, after all, their natural mother. Come as a woman to defend women, and grant that men remain men, as they were born to be. At the very start of this debate I call as witness of the truth of my words the primordial mother, original source of all creation, the sacred nature of the universe, she who united the elements of the world – earth, air, fire and water – and through their mingling wrought all living creatures.

She knew we were a meld of perishable stuffs, granted an all too short existence, and made it so that the death of one would be the birth of another, and that procreation would keep mortality in check, one life sending forth another in infinite succession. Because a thing cannot be born of a single source, to each species she granted the two genders: to the male she gave the seed principle, and she shaped the female into a vessel for that seed. She draws them together by means of desire and unites one to the other in accordance with the healthy requirement of need, so that, each remaining within its natural bounds, the woman will not pretend improbably to have become a man, nor will the man wax indecently effeminate. Thus it is that the unions of men with women have perpetuated to this day the human race through an undying chain of inheritance, instead of some man claiming the glory of being uniquely the product of another man. Quite the contrary, all honor two names as equally respectable, for all have a mother and at the same time a father.

In the beginning, when men were imbued with feelings worthy of heroes, they honored the virtue that makes us akin to the gods; they obeyed the laws fixed by nature and, conjoined with a woman of fitting age, they became fathers of virtuous children. But little by little the race fell from those heights into the abyss of lust, seeking pleasure along new and errant paths. Finally, lechery, overstepping all bounds, transgressed the very laws of nature. Moreover, how could the man who first eyed his peer as though a woman not have resorted to tyrannical violence, or deceit? Two beings of one sex met in one bed; when they looked at one another they blushed neither at what they did to each other, nor at what each suffered to be done to him. Sowing their seed (as the saying goes) upon barren rocks, they traded slight delight for great disgrace.

Nerve and tyranny have gone so far as to mutilate nature with a sacrilegious steel, discovering, by ripping from males their very manhood, a way to prolong their use. However, in order to remain like young boys, these unfortunates are no longer men. They are nothing but ambiguous enigmas of dual gender, having lost the one into which they were born, but not having attained the one they aspired to. The flower of childhood, having thus lingered a while into their youth, wilts into a premature old age. But we still count as boys those already old, for they know not real maturity. Thus vile lust, mistress of all evils, contriving ever more shameful pleasures and stooping eagerly to any baseness, has slid all the way to the vice that cannot decently be mentioned.

If all obeyed the laws given us by Providence, relations with women would satisfy us, and the world would be washed clean of all crime. Animals can not corrupt anything through depravity, so the

...lunging hungrily for the young...

law of nature remains unpolluted. Male lions do not get excited over
other male lions, and when in rut, Aphrodite awakens their desires
for females. The bull, master of his herd, mounts the cows; the ram
fills all the sheep with his male seed. What else? The boars, do they
not cover the sows in their sty? The wolves, do they not mix with
she-wolves? To sum it up, neither the birds who ride the winds, nor
the fishes fated to their wet element, nor the animals on land, seek
dealings with other males: for them the decrees of Providence remain
inviolate. But you men of overrated wisdom, you truly debased
beasts, what novel raving drives you to rise up against the laws and

commit a double crime? What blind insensibility blankets your souls, to doubly stray from the good road, fleeing what you should chase and chasing what you should flee? If everyone did likewise there would be no one left!

Socrates' disciples wield truly admirable arguments with which they fool young boys, not yet in full possession of their reason, but anyone favored with a grain of sense can hardly be swayed by them. They feign love of the soul and, as if ashamed to love the beauty of the body, style themselves "lovers of virtue." Often I had a good laugh over that. How is it, O venerable philosophers, that you dismiss with such disdain those whose age has long since proven their worth, and whose gray hairs vouch for their virtue? How come your love, so full of wisdom, lunges hungrily for the young, whose judgement is not yet fully formed, and who know not which road to take? Is there some law that taints lack of beauty as perverse, and decrees the beautiful as always good and praiseworthy? Yet, to quote Homer, that great prophet of truth:

> One man may fail to impress us with his looks
> But a god can crown his words with beauty, charm,
> And men look on with delight when he speaks out.
> Never faltering, filled with winning self-control,
> He shines forth at assembly grounds and people gaze
> At him like a god when he walks through the streets.[2]

And elsewhere he also said:

> No sense in your head to match your handsome looks.[3]

Indeed, prudent Ulysses is favored over beautiful Nireus.

How is it that your love does not pursue prudence, or justice, or the other virtues which upon occasion crown maturity? Why is the beauty of the young the only thing that inflames your ardent passions? Ought one to have loved Phaedrus, betrayer of Lysias, O Plato? Was it right to love the virtues of Alcibiades, who mutilated the statues of the gods and revealed the Eleusinian mysteries between cups of wine? Who would confess to being his lover when he fled Athens to make his stand in Decelea and openly aspired to tyranny? As long as he remained beardless, according to the divine Plato, he was loved by all, but as soon as he became a man and his intellect, previously unripe, reached its full dimension, he was hated by all. Why is that? It is because the men who call "virtue" the beauty of the body put an honorable label on a shameful affection, and are rather lovers of children than lovers of wisdom.[4] But to avoid recalling the famous only to besmirch them, I will not speak further of these matters.

Let's now descend from these lofty considerations to an examination of your own lusts, Callicratidas; I will demonstrate that the use of women is better far than that of boys. To start, I deem enjoyment to be more satisfying the longer it continues. Fleeting delight ends, as they say, before it has begun. Real pleasure lies in what is lasting. Would that it had pleased the gods for stingy Fate to spin long the thread of our life, granting enjoyment of perpetual health with no foothold for grief. Then we would spend our days in feasts and celebrations. But since some nefarious demon has begrudged us such great boons, the sweetest of real pleasures are those that last. And woman, from maidenhood until her middle years, before the wrinkles of old age have carved her face, is worthy indeed of commerce with men and, even when her beauty is gone,

With wiser tongue
Experience speaks,
Than can the young.[5]

Furthermore, one who courts boys of twenty seems to me a seeker of passive pleasures, a votary of an ambivalent Aphrodite. The bodies of those become men are hard, their chins, once soft, have become bristly, and their muscular thighs are soiled by hairs. As for what is most hidden, I leave that knowledge to you, men of experience. Any woman's skin, however, shines with grace. Thick locks crown her head like the purple flower of the hyacinth – some spilling down her back to embellish her shoulders, others framing the ears and the temples, curlier than parsley in a field. Her entire body, devoid of the least hair, has, as has been said, more brilliance than amber, or glass from Sidon.

Why not seek, when it comes to desires, those which are mutual, and which satisfy alike the one who gives and the one who receives? We do not like, in truth, to lead solitary lives as the dumb beasts do, but rather, joined by our mutual feelings, we find our happiness greater and our pains lighter when shared. Hence the invention of the communal table, brought out as the center of a gathering of friends. If we grant our belly the pleasure it demands, we will not, for

Girl dancer

example, drink Thasian wine by ourselves, nor stuff ourselves in solitude with fancy dishes. Each finds more pleasant what he shares with another, and, likewise, we prefer reciprocal enjoyments. One unites with a woman in mutual desire; the two part equally satisfied one with the other after tasting the same delights, unless we are to believe Tiresias, who claimed the woman's pleasure far surpasses the man's. I consider, therefore, that men should value not the selfish pleasure they can take, but the one they can afford in exchange. Nobody in his right mind would claim that is the case with boys: the lover gets up and leaves, having tasted joys beyond compare, but his victim begins with pains and tears. Even later, when, I am told, his suffering grows less acute, you will never be anything but a bother to him, because of pleasure he has none. If we can speak more freely, as suits the woodlands of Aphrodite, I will say, Callicratidas, that it is allowed to make use of a woman in the fashion of a boy, the road being open to a double enjoyment, but the male must never lend himself to effeminate delights.

That is why, if a woman can satisfy the lover of boys, let him abstain from the latter; or else, if males can conjoin with males, then from now on allow women also to love each other. Come, men of the new age, you legislators of strange thrills: having blazed fresh trails for men's pleasures, grant women the same license. Let them commingle as do the males: let a woman, girded with those obscene implements, monstrous toys of sterility, lie with another woman, just as a man with another man. Let those filthy lesbians, word that only rarely reaches my ears because modesty forbids it, triumph freely. Let our schools for girls be nothing but the domain of Philenis, dishonored by androgynous loves. And yet, would it not be better to see a woman play the man than to see a man take on the role of a woman?

LYCINUS: Having uttered these words with fire and conviction, Charicles grew quiet, his gaze still terrible, almost ferocious. He seemed to have made a conjuration to atone for all male loves. As for me, I glanced at the Athenian with a gentle smile and said, "I had thought, Callicratidas, that I would merely be judging some game, or lark, but here I find myself, due to Charicles' vehemence, referee over a more serious cause. He has grown heated beyond measure, as if on the Areopagus, pleading for a murderer, or a criminal arsonist, or, by Zeus, for an affair of poison. It is time now to make recourse to Athena's help: may the eloquence of Pericles and the tongues of the ten orators marshaled against the Macedonians make your harangue worthy of those declaimed on the Pnyx!" (Continued on page 75)

Zeus and Ganymede

Zeus and Ganymede

On the wide plain at the feet of Mount Ida, the sky and the water met and made love. King Tros, the king of Heaven's grandson, fell for the daughter of the river god and lay in her arms. In time, she grew heavy with child and gave life to a golden-haired boy. They named him Ganymede, and how they adored that child! Tros had boundless wealth and power — he even stamped his name on the land and its people — but all his riches were as chaff to him, compared to his son. He posted handpicked men to watch over Ganymede, told them in no uncertain terms to keep an eye on him at all times. Under their watchful gaze the prince grew into a strapping youth and a hunter without equal. He spent his days hiking with his friends through the mountains, setting his hounds on the heels of antlered stags, and debating with his tutors.

Ganymede had won fame, but not in battle, nor in the contests of strength. His shape alone had made him famous, for he was the most handsome born of the race of men. Whenever he and his friends took to the streets of Troy, Ganymede turned the heads of all the townsfolk;

10

20

Zeus

they all fell for his stunning, god-like beauty. Even the eye of Zeus king of the gods lingered upon the prince. The more Zeus looked at Ganymede, the brighter the fire of his love burned. Finally, heedless of his wife Hera's jealous rages and unable to resist the boy's thighs, he hatched a plan to win the young Trojan.

Ganymede

The god first shed his form, and took the shape of that eagle who carries his thunderbolts. Then he unleashed a terrifying thunderstorm, plunging all Troy into darkness. Zeus winged down into the black clouds coiling about the peaks of Ida, sending shafts of lightning stabbing every which way. Ganymede's guardians raced for shelter, falling

30

47

over each other in their haste. Amid the turmoil, the massive eagle swooped unseen out of the clouds. He pounced and caught up the awestruck Ganymede in his talons. He set the boy on his back, launched himself once more upon the wind, and Ganymede hung on for dear life. The guardians raced back, reaching for the clouds; the hounds leaped, barking madly at the sky, all in vain. The god beat the air with powerful wings once, twice, and the storm swallowed him up.

Zeus flew beyond the clouds, lost himself into the deep blue sky, and the boy clung in wonder to his plumes. At last the eagle set down and folded his wings, and Ganymede found himself in bright Olympus. He looked around, dazzled by this new world, but the eagle wrapped a friendly wing around his shoulder, looked him in the eye, and let him know that from now on he would walk among the immortals and serve them at their table. At feast times it would fall to him to mull the red nectar, draw it from its golden mixing bowl into a golden pitcher, and pour each god his portion. Hebe, Zeus' and Hera's own daughter, had served the drinks till now, but Zeus brought up that she once stumbled, mocked her for being a clumsy oaf, and sent her packing to make room for his friend.

Hera was fit to be tied. Livid with rage, she turned on Zeus, shrieking, berating him for bringing that horrid, long-haired mortal into Olympus, for wronging her innocent daughter. Zeus gave as good as he got, threw in her face that he liked the boy's kisses. He kept the blond prince as his beloved and took him to his bed.

Hera raged on, but all the other immortals honored the son of Tros for his beauty — just one glimpse of him brought them pure joy. In Olympus, Ganymede lacked for nothing. Zeus looked after him well, and made him immortal. Nor was Ganymede lonely — he and young Eros became bosom buddies. Every chance they got, the boys went off by themselves, casting dice for hours on end, but Eros was way too sly a player: he beat Ganymede every time, left him penniless and in tears.   70

Ever since King Tros saw his best men shuffle down from the hills empty-handed; ever since he heard from their lips the boy had been stolen, grief beyond all measure had filled his heart. He wept bitter tears, desperate to know where the heaven-sent whirlwind had carried his son. He forgot sleep, forgot food, and mourned the boy night and day. Zeus saw his suffering and took pity on the man. He hurried down a winged herald to inform the king his son was like a true god now, deathless and forever young. Zeus also counted out rich payment, in trade for snatching   80 Ganymede: A grapevine of glinting gold that always bears fruit, and a brace of prancing stallions, the finest beneath the dawn, the same that carry the immortals. When Tros learned of his son's glory, he rejoiced and hung up his mourning garb. He drove his storm-footed horses as fast as the wind, all his sorrow now turned to joy.

Hera, however, still seethed with jealousy. She hankered for revenge, but thundering Zeus was far too strong for her to tackle. So the goddess went after the Trojans instead, seared *them* with her anger. In the end, she fanned the   90

flames of war and all Greece rose up to do her bidding, massacred Ganymede's kin and the whole Trojan race to boot. But Ganymede himself was beyond her reach. Zeus had set the boy among the stars as Aquarius, the water bearer, shielded him under the wings of the Eagle, and made sure his fame would echo down the centuries.

Zeus and Ganymede

Hercules and Hylas

We are not the first mortals to see beauty in what is beautiful. No, even Hercules, who defeated the savage Nemean lion, once loved a lad — sweet Hylas — whose hair still hung down in curls. But disaster often strikes the careless lover.

One day Hercules was trudging, together with his wife and little son, over a rocky mountain trail. Their provisions had long ago run out and there were no others to be had, for they were crossing the wild country of Thiodamas, king of the savage Dryopians. The little boy had stepped on a thorn so his father was carrying him, but the child, full of complaint, now raged with hunger. At last they ran across a farmer, old before his time, ploughing the earth with a brace of shambling oxen, a stout ten-foot pole in his hand, and a bulging satchel slung from his shoulder. Hercules was filled with joy to see another man: "Hail, father, may all your prayers be answered. Hercules is my name, and I bid you, if you can spare a crust of bread to dull the child's hunger, bring it out! I'll always remember your friendly gift." It did not occur to him the ploughman was Thiodamas himself, nor had that yokel king ever heard of any Hercules: "Be gone from my sight while you still can, you vagabond, whoever you may be! Hungry have you come

Hercules and his son

Hercules and the ox

and hungry will you cross my plough," the peasant shot
back, and whacked Hercules sharply with his pole.

Hercules' blood boiled. Not for nothing was he the
strongest man in the world. He yanked the pole out of
the king's grasp, snapped it over his knee like a twig, then
shoved the man aside and unyoked one of the oxen, his
favorite food of all. Thiodamas sputtered with rage. Never
had anyone dared cross him like this. He filled the air with
a stream of curses foul enough to shrivel a lesser man, and
stormed off to call his people to arms, turning time and
again to lob rock after rock at Hercules, who shrugged off
the stones like so many gnats. With his sharp bronze sword
he made short work of the lumbering ox, then skewered
the meat, roasted it to a turn, and pulled it off the fire.
They all fell to and ate their fill, but Hercules put away
the most by far, didn't even spare the bones.

As they were polishing off the last of the meal, King
Thiodamas rode up with a host of his warriors, all armed
to the teeth. His men would dispatch the bum right off,

thought the king, and sent only two fighters forward. Hercules, however, swung his huge carved club, tossing the burly warriors right and left like rag dolls. The king could not believe his eyes and sent out more and more fighters. However, as many as stepped up to do battle with him, so many Hercules overcame. Thiodamas, beside himself, decided to take matters into his own hands. He lunged out with his spear, but Hercules dodged the thrust and pounded *50* the king's life out with one swift blow. The Dryopians, fed up with bloodshed, sued for peace. They pledged undying loyalty to Hercules and set before him Thiodamas' own son as token of good faith. He was a lanky country boy with a curly blond mane reaching to his shoulders, who went by the name of Hylas. Hercules was struck by his looks. He agreed to take on the youth, and appointed him weapons bearer.

Hylas had little love in his heart for the man who killed his father, but he could not help admiring Hercules' strength. Working by his new master's side day in, day out, *60* he grew proud to sling Hercules' great bow and quiver over his own shoulder, to cook his meals, to learn from him the right way to go about a warrior's life. In turn, Hercules took great care to teach him all he knew and mold him to his liking, so Hylas would attain the true measure of a man. As time went on, the two of them struck up a friendship, and fell in love. From then on they were always together, morning, noon, and at bedtime.

And so they went from adventure to adventure while the years passed like days, and by Hercules' side Hylas *70* became a man. Around the time when the first beard

Hercules and Hylas

began to shade his cheeks, heralds were sent to every city,
inviting all seasoned warriors to sail aboard the Argo in
quest of the Golden Fleece. There was none abler than
Hercules, and Jason himself, the leader of the expedition,
sought him out and begged him to lend a hand. Not
about to miss out on such a glorious undertaking,
Hercules consented. He set aside his labors and joined
the crew and, naturally, brought Hylas along. Once
aboard, Hercules thrilled to meet his old comrade,   *80*
Polyphemus. Soon, a fair wind rose and the heroes made
sail and got underway. Hera queen of Heaven herself had
sent down the breeze. She doted on Jason and did all in
her power to speed him on his way, to win for Greece that
priceless prize, the fleece of Zeus' winged ram, and
its wool was pure gold.

Late one windless afternoon, after laboring all day at
the oars, the heroes raised the rocky shore of lush Mysia.
Worn out from churning the bitter water, they shipped
oars and moored the sleek black vessel by the mouth of   *90*
the Mysian river. They had come in friendship, so the
Mysians and their sons welcomed them warmly, gave
them the pick of their harvest, and fatted sheep, and
much sweet wine. The heroes right away spread out a
handsome feast. They gathered armfuls of scented herbs
for couches, stirred water into wine in the mixing bowls,
and built a great fire. At nightfall they sacrificed a sheep
to lord Apollo for protection – it was the hour for the
sleepless nymphs to start their revels, those dreaded spirits
who haunt the woods and streams from dusk to dawn.   *100*

Proud Hera, however, had devised her own plans for the heroes. From the day he was born she had pursued Hercules, had made his life miserable. Her husband's cheating drove her wild, but she did not dare go after Zeus himself, he would have crushed her in an instant. Instead she heaped hardships on his bastard son. This time she had picked a nymph and warned her to get ready, for she would send her a man like a god to be her husband.

110 The evening sacrifice over, Hylas picked up a bronze jug and strode off alone into the gathering gloom, in need of fresh water for Hercules' supper. Nor did Hercules himself linger. That very day his massive oar had broken in his hands, and he meant to carve himself a new one on the spot. Wishing the others joy of the feast, he too made his way into the woods, seeking some towering tree to uproot, while Polyphemus seated himself by the path to await his return. Hylas, meanwhile, came upon a marshy hollow, brushed aside the reeds and ferns standing in his way, and found himself before a pure gushing spring. Just

120 below its rippled surface, however, Hera's nymph was lurking. She glimpsed him standing on the shore in the moonlight, and shivers of desire ran through her.

Hylas bent down and dipped the jug to fill it. But as the waters swirled in and the bronze rang loud, the boy noticed neither the splashing nor the shadow of the rising nymph. She reached up, wrapped her arm around his neck, hungry to taste his tender mouth. Then with her other hand she drew him down. He let out a brief, startled shout, and plunged into the flowing stream.

The nymph hugged Hylas tight and swam with him to   *130*
her underwater cave.

Hylas and the nymphs

Even as the nymph vanished into the depths with Hylas,
Polyphemus was racing flat out towards the spring. He had
heard Hylas' cry and feared something was amiss. His keen
ear led him right to the spot, but, besides the bronze jug,
there was no trace of the boy. He dove back into the forest,
and as he searched high and low in the darkness he ran into
Hercules, on his way back to the camp, dragging a massive fir.
"My poor friend, what bitter tidings I have for you," gasped
Polyphemus, all out of breath. "Hylas went to fetch water   *140*
and never made it back. Perhaps bandits made off with him
or beasts are tearing him to pieces; I heard his shout for help."
    As those words sank in, Hercules broke into a cold sweat,
and love, mixed with numb fear, swirled like a whirlwind
through his heart. He hurled the trunk to the ground and

rushed wildly through the woods, frightening the trees and mountains. "Hylas! Hylas! Hylas!" he thundered. His friend called out in answer, but his shout drifted in muffled, as if far away. All night long, Hercules and Polyphemus scoured

150 the slopes and valleys of that unbounded wilderness, forgetting all about their journey. Hera, meanwhile, crowned her work with a howling gale, sent before dawn. Jason and the heroes had to cast off and put to sea to keep the black ship off the rocks, had to leave their best men stranded.

That next day, Hercules rounded up all the Mysians and threatened to lay waste all their land if they did not come up with his boy, dead or alive. Little did he know the nymph had already seduced Hylas, despite himself. He had settled in with her and her sisters in their cavern, eager to share their

160 power and their love. The Mysians, to appease Hercules, picked out the noblest of their sons, and handed the boys over to him as pledges of good faith, swearing a solemn oath they would never give up looking for his friend.

Still Hercules could not rest. He had gone over every inch of that forest, and now he stomped through the lonely woods like a madman, unable to tear himself away. Zeus, seeing the tortures of his son, could bear it no longer. He rounded on Hera and wrecked the life of *her* favorite in revenge, dooming the man's children to die by their own

170 mother's hand. And the goddess shook before his might, aghast to see the wave of sorrow about to break over the head of her beloved Jason.

Moved to pity for Hercules, Zeus then drifted down around him a dew of mystic nectar with the power of deep

and quiet sleep. But even as the outer
eye closes, the inner one awakens.
Hercules beheld Hylas rising from
the water, his supple body wrapped
in a robe of saffron weeds,
the gift of the sly nymph.   180
"Why, father, do you
keep on searching? It's
such a waste of time.
This is my home now,
it is the will of Fate.
That sweet quiver I used
to shoulder — my heart
breaks for it; but it's
time for you to carry on
now. Never fail in your   190
labors, never let the sight
of me fade from your eyes,
always remember our love."
    Tears welled up in
Hercules' eyes: "How can I
leave you here alone, my
darling boy, and we never again
to brave our stupendous
trials together?" He
reached out, hungry
for one more hug,
but his hands only
clawed the mist.

Hercules

Orpheus

Orpheus, the son of the Thracian river god, lived with his parents in a cave deep in the primeval forest. When the boy came of age, his father whispered to him the secret teachings of Dionysus, the god of wine. His mother, Calliope, the Muse of song, filled Orpheus with inspiration, and such songs began to flow from his mouth that even the gods on high stopped and turned to listen.

Apollo lord of the lyre was drunk with pleasure to hear Orpheus' music. He swept down from bright Olympus and took the golden-voiced mortal as his boyfriend. The god taught him to master the lyre, so he might accompany his singing, and time stood still when they were together. All too soon the day came when Apollo had to leave, but, as they parted, he offered Orpheus his lyre as a love gift. Orpheus spent all the livelong day learning the stories of the gods, and before long he could sing every last one. Thirsty for knowledge, he even traveled to the sandy shores of Egypt to study the secrets of the Underworld. Upon his return, all the Greeks bowed down to him as the greatest among them in knowledge and wisdom, as well as music.

Dionysus upon a Satyr

The more Orpheus learned, the more he was saddened by the cruel ways of the people of his land. Those forest-dwelling Thracians were men without pity. When they made offerings to the gods, they dragged children onto the altars, lifted their flint knives, and fouled the gods' houses with human blood. In their dealings with men, they were ruthless and war-like. In their hunts they butchered all the beasts in sight, emptied the forests of life. Orpheus made up his mind to put an end to all this savagery. He took up

30   his lyre and set out to instruct the men of his land, to tame them with music. From him the Thracians learned to give up bloody sacrifice and honor the gods with fragrant smoke instead, learned to set their weapons down before crossing the thresholds of temples. He also taught them to respect all creatures and not to touch living food. To ease their hard lives, Orpheus revealed the mysteries of Dionysus, he who makes men free, and the blessings of the grape. Above all, Orpheus opened their eyes to the power of love. He was the first to teach them the art of loving

40   boys: to devote themselves to the young, and so to savor the flower of their youth.

Change, however, does not come easily to a brutal land. There were many who rose up against Orpheus and his teachings, none so fiercely as the women of Thrace. They had many reasons to be aggrieved, for Orpheus not only led their husbands astray, but took away the boys they loved as well. To top it off, he let only the men witness Dionysus' temple mysteries. The women he sent off to the forests instead, there to be handmaidens to the god, to honor him

Orpheus and the Thracians

50 and his satyrs in sacred drunken dances which no man may witness. But the women of Thrace were wounded to the quick for being booted from the temple. They plotted cruel vengeance against the prophet, and only fear of their husbands stayed their hands. Orpheus, however, paid them no mind. He went on singing the gods' stories to his people, edging them away from their rough ways.

Maenad and Satyrs

Orpheus yearned to spread his teachings to the ends of the world, so when heralds dropped by looking for volunteers to bring back the Golden Fleece from the far
60 reaches of the sea, he seized the chance. In his youth, his parents had never pressed him to join his mates in war games, but his lack of skill with weapons did not stop him. He shouldered his lyre and struck out for the seashore,

where the black ship Argo was poised, ready for launching.
When the other crewmen saw him draw near, equipped
with a lyre instead of sharp weapons, they took him for a
weakling and had no use for him. Seers, however, warned
them to beware, for without Orpheus not one of them
would make it back alive. From the very start he proved
his mettle: When time came for the Argo to slip her ways,   70
some of the Argonauts put their shoulders to the stern,
others strained against thick cables made fast to the prow,
but the ship would not budge an inch through the thick
sand. But no sooner did Orpheus pluck the strings of his
lyre, that she glided by herself into the waters and bobbed
there patiently, waiting for them to board.

Thus, when the Argo unfolded her fans of oars and put
to sea, Orpheus, too, was aboard, setting the pace for the
oarsmen with his music. In time, the crew grew to prize
him for his talents, and they were dear to him too, Calais   80
above all, that tawny-winged son of the Thracian North
Wind. The boy was always taking to the air, mischievous,
swooping down on the most handsome of the sailors,
stealing kisses on the sly. In the end, as the seers had
foretold, so it came to pass. Orpheus' magic overcame
danger after danger, and when the prize was finally in
sight, his music again saved the day: Upon hearing the
harmonious twang of his lyre, the guardian dragon of
the Fleece curled up and fell asleep. At last, when they
again set foot upon the rocky shores of Greece, the men   90
scattered, each to his own hearth, and Orpheus, too,
hurried to his father's cave and to the land he loved.

The Bard

Back in Thrace, he once again took to roaming the forests, singing his god-songs and love-songs as he went. His music was more entrancing than ever: unshiftable mountain boulders tumbled meekly after him now, the winds stopped in mid-flight, and ancient oaks pulled up their roots and danced round and round. One day, Orpheus came face to face with a lovely green-eyed dryad, Eurydice by name, and from that moment she was always *100* in his thoughts. She, too, kept after him to play his music and liven up the dryads' dances. Before long, a wedding was arranged. Everyone came, even the god of marriage, but his torch burned dim, poured out billows of choking smoke, and soon he took wing and sped away. The next day, while Eurydice was running through a meadow, she stepped on a stout viper. It wheeled and struck, pumping its venom deep into her ankle. Her death was painful and quick. Orpheus was gripped with a deep desire to die with her. The following day, however, he summoned up his strength, shouldered his *110* lyre, and set out for the Underworld to reclaim his beloved. He was raring to take on the nether gods: he knew all their secrets, surely he could tame their cruelty.

He came upon the entrance to the House of Death and descended, ever deeper, into the bowels of the earth. His songs charmed all the monsters and guardians he met along the way, even fierce Charon, who rowed him across the cascading waters of the Styx, black river of death. At last he stood before the dark gods. He took up his lyre and plied them with his music. He sang of his love for Eurydice, and *120* pleaded for her release. His melody echoed throughout the great vaulted caves and the Underworld ground to a halt, as all the souls and demons crowded round to hear him play. Even the shade of Eurydice limped up to Hades' throne. "We are defeated," groaned the mighty lord of the Underworld. He pointed to Eurydice's shade: "You may follow in his footsteps." Then he turned to Orpheus: "And you, lest you lose her forever, turn not to look upon her until bright day reveals the gods of Heaven, and the gates

130 of the Underworld have been left behind!"

Higher and higher, through arching caverns wreathed in mist they slogged, Orpheus in front, Eurydice following the sound of his lyre, and Hermes shadowing them both, unseen, to watch they did not flout Hades' command. Finally, just as Orpheus broke through to open air, a mad thought grabbed him: What if Hades had tricked him after all? He halted and spun around. There was Eurydice, right behind him, about to step into the sunlight. But Hermes laid his hand on her, stopped her in her tracks, drew her

140 back into the darkness. Orpheus had but a moment to lift her veil aside, and to look into her eyes this one last time.

After Eurydice died her second death, Orpheus could not bear to look at another woman. He sought refuge in the temple of Apollo, the god who once had loved him, and became his priest. Even his music was different now: He no longer praised the love of women, but sang only the beauty of youths instead. Those women who still made eyes at him, he spurned without fail. The pent-up rage of the Thracian wives came back redoubled, but Orpheus, as before, gave

150 them no thought. His mind was on Calais, his friend from

Orpheus, Eurydice, and Hermes

the Argo, whom he loved best of all the boys — he had a true passion for that lad. Oftentimes he'd lounge in the shade of an old tree, serenading his friend. And on those rare nights when Calais was not bedded down by his side, Orpheus tossed restlessly till dawn, tormented by loneliness.

The killing of Orpheus

Spring came round, and with it, the feast of Dionysus.
Orpheus and the men shuttered themselves inside the
temple, while the women trampled through the forests of
the night, disheveled, drunk. In their frenzy they stumbled
160 upon the temple gates. There was Orpheus inside with their
men, gathered around the altar. The women's hate burst its
banks and the fumes of the wine made them forget all fear.
They took up weapons from the pile by the door, barged
into the temple, killed all who stood in their way, and tore
Orpheus limb from limb. His remains they scattered all
over the surrounding meadows, then they kneeled by the
river bank to wash off the bloodstains. The stream, however,

refused to lend its waters to cleanse their crime. It chose to
dive underground, where it still runs. The men of Thrace
were overwhelmed with sadness to see their prophet   *170*
murdered, and turned on their women to punish them.
They held back from bloodshed, however. Instead, they
tattooed their wives' arms and legs, that way they might look
upon the marks and not forget the foul deed all their days.

Calliope and the Muses rushed down in tears, gathered
up Orpheus' limbs, and laid them to rest. The river,
however, kept his head and lyre and floated them
downstream, still singing, until they reached the foaming
breakers of the sea. There, the winds and waves bore them
across to sacred Lesbos, the island which ever since has been   *180*
possessed by love and song. The men of Lesbos buried the
head with honors, and the Muses, by Zeus' leave, studded
the lyre with stars and flung it into the heavens. On Earth,
too, Orpheus' legacy lives on, and across the hills of Thrace
the love of handsome boys flourishes to this day.

Dionysus and Satyrs

73

Eros

Different Loves

Lycinus continues his account to Theomnestes with his own words of encouragement to Callicratidas, the lover of boys, who is about to speak in defense of male love.

Part III

LYCINUS: "May the eloquence of Pericles and the tongues of the ten orators marshaled against the Macedonians make your harangue worthy of those declaimed on the Pnyx!" Callicratidas collected his thoughts a moment or two. Judging by his expression, he too seemed ready for combat. Then he launched into his rebuttal.

CALLICRATIDAS: If women took part in government meetings, in the courts, and in public affairs, you surely would be a general, Charicles, or president, and they would raise bronze statues of you in the public squares. In fact, the wisest among them, were they to speak in favor of their cause, could hardly have outdone you — neither Telesilla, who fought against the Spartiates and in whose honor, at Argos, Mars is deemed one of the gods of women; nor Sappho, that sweet glory of Lesbos; nor Theano, daughter of wise Pythagoras. It may even be that Pericles defended Aspasia with less eloquence. But if men are now to speak on behalf of women, then let us men speak on behalf of men. And you, Aphrodite, grant me favor, for we too honor Eros, your son!

I had thought our argument would remain on friendly footing, but since Charicles in his speech started theorizing on behalf of women, I will gladly seize the opportunity to tell him this: only male love is the product of both desire *and* virtue. I would have wished, had it been possible, that we stood beneath the plane tree that once heard the speeches of Socrates — happier tree than the Academy or the Lycaeum — and under which Phaedrus lounged, as the divine man, best beloved of the Graces, tells us. From its branches, like those of the talking oak of Dodona, we would hear a voice defending the love of boys, in memory of young Phaedrus. Alas, that cannot be, "for between us lie shadowy mountain ranges, seas that surge and thunder."[1]

We have halted here, strangers in a foreign land, and Cnidus is the domain of Charicles. However, I will not succumb to fear. But come you to my aid, divine spirit, protector of friendship, revealer of its mysteries, Eros. Not the mischievous child drawn by the hands of painters, but He who was made perfect from birth by the first principle of the seed. *You* are the one, in fact, who formed the universe, until then shapeless, dark and confused. Pulling the world as if out of a grave, you pushed back all-enveloping Chaos and flung him into the deepest abyss of Tartarus, where truly "iron gates and brazen thresholds loom,"[2] so that he may never return from the prison where he is chained. Then, beating back the night with your dazzling light, you became the creator of all things, animate and inanimate. You have inspired in men, by means of the lofty sentiment of harmony, the noble passions of friendship, so that a soul still innocent and tender, nurtured in the shade of goodwill, will ripen into maturity.

Marriage is a solution devised by the demands of procreation, but male love alone must rule the heart of a philosopher. Everything fashioned uniquely for luxury is valued far above what arises from need, and everywhere people prefer the beautiful to the merely useful. As long as men were ignorant and lacked the ease for seeking something beyond the fruit of their daily toil, they deemed themselves content with bare necessities – they had no time to discover a better way of life. But once urgent needs were satisfied, the men who followed were free from the shackles of necessity and able to improve things; the whole gradual development of the sciences and of the arts that we see today is one interesting result. The first men were hardly born, before they had to seek a remedy for daily hunger. Caught by these pressing needs, and deprived by poverty of the freedom to pursue refinements, they subsisted on roots and herbs, or, above all, on the fruit of the oak. But shortly thereafter these foods were relegated to the beasts, and the farmers toiled to sow wheat and oats, which they had noticed grew anew each year. No one is so mad as to claim the acorn is tastier than grain.

Furthermore, in ancient times did men not cloak themselves in
the pelts of flayed animals? Did they not seek refuge from cold in
mountain caves, or in the hollows of old stumps, or in the trunks
of dead trees? But leaving behind little by little these primitive ways,
they wove wool, built houses, and, imperceptibly, the art of these
various crafts, with time for teacher, produced beautiful lace in place
of simple cloth and lofty roofs instead of simple cabins. Magnificent
stonework was erected and the sad nakedness of the walls was
painted in flowery colors. Thus these arts and sciences, once mute
and sunk in oblivion, shone bright after their sleep. Each artist
handed down his invention to his successor, and each descendant
added his own to this heritage, filling out what was lacking.

Let us not expect male love from these ancient times; men had
to conjoin with women so that the race would not die out for lack
of seed. Manifold wisdom and the virtuous desires, fueled by love
of the beautiful, could only come to light in a century that has left
nothing unexplored; thus love of youths has blossomed together
with divine philosophy. Therefore, Charicles, do not condemn as
evil everything not invented long ago, and do not disdain the love
of boys just because dealings with women have an older pedigree.
Let's remember that the very first discoveries were prompted by
need, but those arising from progress are only the better for it,
and worthier of our esteem.

I could barely stifle my laughter when I heard Charicles praise
the beasts and the barren wastes of the Scythians – in the heat of
the argument he seemed almost sorry to be Greek. Unconcerned
about undermining his own argument, he did not hide his thoughts
by speaking in low tones. Quite the contrary, he raised his voice and
fairly roared: "Neither lions, nor bears, nor boars love another male,
but their desires drive them solely towards their females." What's so
amazing about that? What man chooses by dint of reason, animals
cannot, for they are too stupid to think. If Prometheus or some
other god had endowed them with human reason, they would not
be living in the desert or the forest and they would not be devouring
each other, but, like us, they would build temples, gather around the
hearth in houses, and subject themselves to common laws. Animals
are condemned by their own nature to miss out on the providential

gifts afforded by intellect. Is it any wonder that they should be deprived, among other things, of male love? Lions do not love each other, but they are not philosophers; bears do not love each other, but they have no understanding of the beauty of friendship. Among men however, wisdom joined with knowledge, choosing, after numerous trials, what it found most beautiful, has decreed that male loves are the most sound.

So, Charicles, spare me these lectures more befitting the wanton lives of courtesans. Don't insult our dignity and modesty in such crude terms, and do not make out Divine Eros to be a little fool. Consider, though it is late to educate oneself at your age, consider now, since you have not done so before, that Eros is a double god. He does not always arrive by the same path, nor does he always excite the same desires in our souls. One, I would say, is a ceaseless prankster. No reason governs him – he inhabits the souls of the foolish, and from him come the yearnings for women. He is the one who inspires rapes, for he pushes with irresistible force towards that which we crave. But the other Eros, father of the Ogygian age,[3] that honest and profoundly sacred vision, is the propagator of healthy desires, and fills the souls with sweetness. Under the protection of this god, we taste pleasure mixed with virtue. As the tragic poet once said, love has two breaths, and two completely different passions bear the same name. Shame also is a twofold goddess, simultaneously good and evil:

> Shame can good and evil weave alike
> And men in warring camps divide.
> For the first she can't be praised too highly
> From the bottom of our hearts we blame her for the other.[4]

So it is not at all surprising if, passion having taken the name of virtue, we should call Eros both unbridled lust as well as temperate affection.

CHARICLES: Is marriage nothing then, and shall we banish the race of women? How will men ever perpetuate themselves?

...choosing what it found most beautiful...

CALLICRATIDAS: In the words of the all-wise Euripides: "It will be better, rather than have dealings with women, to go into the temples and the sacred places and purchase children in exchange for gold and silver, so as to assure our posterity."[5] In truth, necessity burdens us under her heavy yoke, and forces us to obey. If, on one hand, thanks to intellect, we opt for the beautiful, then, on the other, let the useful yield to the needful. Let there be women for making children, but as for the rest, I will have none of it. What sane man could stand a woman who, from morning on, bedecks herself with strange artifices? Her true figure is devoid of beauty, and she covers up the indecencies of nature with borrowed ornaments.

Music lesson

If we were to see women as they rose from bed we would consider them uglier than those animals it is thought unlucky to mention before noontime – I speak of the monkeys. That is why they lock themselves in and do not wish to be seen by any man. A gaggle of servants, young and old, equal to them in beauty, swarms around offering up to the disagreeable face all sorts of pomades. They do not, after the sloth of sleep, refresh their mistress with a splash of clear water, then to move on to serious concerns. No, they merely lend, by means of cosmetics, a dash of color to an unpleasant aspect. Just as in public processions, each has her function: One holds a silver plate, another a pincushion, a mirror, a host of little boxes as in a drugstore, vases filled with a thousand secret poisons for whitening teeth or blackening eyelids.

But it is the care of the hair, above all, that takes the most time. Some, by means of concoctions which make the curls shine brighter than the noonday sun, dye them as if wool and turn them blond, making them lose their natural tint. Others, imagining themselves more beautiful with black hair, spend their husbands' wealth on that, and reek of all Arabia. The iron heated over glowing embers will curl even the most unruly hair, so that the forehead, rimmed with waves to the very eyebrows, is only glimpsed through a narrow opening, while in back their tresses drape magnificently over their shoulders.

Next, they put on flower-colored shoes that cut into the flesh and pinch their feet. To keep from appearing totally naked they drape on veils light as air, but whatever these may hide stands out even more than their faces; only women with ugly breasts wrap them in nets. Why bother listing here their spendthrift ways? Those Eritrean pearls hanging from their earlobes, worth many a talent; those serpents twisted about their wrists and arms, would they were real and not golden! Crowns star-studded with Indian gems circle their foreheads, rich necklaces hang from their necks; the gold must abase itself even to their feet to wrap what shows of their heels – it would be better to put their legs in irons. After the whole body, through some kind of witchcraft, has traded in its bastard ugliness for an ersatz beauty, they redden their shameless cheeks with makeup, so as to spruce up their oily skins with a splash of purple.

How do they behave, after all these preparations? They promptly leave the house, and all the gods take their side against the husbands. The women have, in fact, such gods as wretched men do not even know their names. They are, I believe, Coliades, Genetylides, or that Phrygian goddess whose ceremonies commemorate her unfortunate love for a shepherd.[6] Later they go to unspeakable initiations, to suspicious mysteries that exclude men. But I will not reveal any further the corruption of their souls. Upon their return they take interminable baths, then they sit down to sumptuous meals and ply their men with come-ons. When their gluttony has had its fill and they can no longer stuff their mouths, they daintily finger the foods brought before them, talking among themselves about their nights, their multi-colored dreams, and about their beds, filled with such feminine softness that one needs a bath immediately upon rising.

That is how the more tranquil among them live. But if we look closely at those less staid, we would curse Prometheus, all the while reciting Menander's lament:

> Prometheus, is justice not well served
> To the Caucasian rock to have you bound?
> The firebrand to mortals you did give,
> But now in the hate of the gods you live,
> Reward for placing women on the ground.
> Men marry, alas, they tie the knot!
> And then come secret passions, the whole lot.
> When cheating in the marriage bed lies down,
> From it poisons rise, and jealous torment:
> Such are the gifts of womankind to men.[7]

Who would seek such boons? Who would enjoy such a miserable life?

It is only fair now to contrast a boy's manly conduct to that of these foul women. Rising early from his lonely bed he splashes clean water over his eyes, still veiled by the night's sleep, then pins his sacred mantle over his shoulder with a clasp. He leaves his father's house with downcast eyes, not staring at the passers by. He is escorted by his stalwart slaves and tutors, carrying the sacred implements of virtue: not combs with close-set teeth to caress his hair, nor mirrors where shapes reflect as in a portrait, but many-leaved writing tablets, or scrolls relating the virtues of olden days, or, if bound for his music master, his melodious lyre.

After having tempered his mind with philosophical teachings and nourished his soul with all sorts of knowledge, he develops his body with noble athletics. He studies up on Thessalian horses, and, his youth once tamed, he makes use of peace to ready for war, hurling spears and javelins with a sure hand. Then come the games of the palestra.[8] Glistening with oil, he wrestles in the dust under the searing noonday sun, his sweat streaming. Then a quick bath and a frugal meal allow him shortly to resume his activities. Anew his tutors return to relate to him the ancient deeds, engraving in his memory the heroes who distinguished themselves by their courage, prudence, restraint, or fairness. After thus watering his soul with the

dew of these virtues, evening brings his labors to an end. He
metes out the tribute demanded by his stomach, and then sleeps
surrounded by dreams all the sweeter for that his rest follows the
toils of the day.

Who would not be the lover of such a youth? Who so blind of
sight, or dense of mind? How could one not love him, a Hermes at
the palestra, an Apollo with his lyre, as fine a horseman as Castor,
manifesting divine virtues in a mortal body. As for me, heavenly gods,
may my life eternally be spent seated before such a friend, hearing his
gentle voice up close, sharing with him in all things! A lover would
wish to see him reach, after joyful years, an old age free of ills,
without ever having felt the spite of Fate. But if, as is the wont of
human nature, he is laid low by sickness, I would ail with him; and
should he put to a stormy sea, I would sail with him; and if a
powerful tyrant should cast him in irons, I would be chained with
him. Whoever hates him would be my enemy, and I would love those
who wish him well. If I were to see bandits or enemies fall upon him,
I would take up my weapons and fight with my last ounce of strength.
If he were to die, I could not bear to live. My last wish to those
dearest to me after him would be that one grave be dug for us both,
and our bones be mixed so none could tell apart our dumb ashes.

Nor is my love for those worthy of it the first one written down.
The heroes who were close to the gods thought up this law, whereby
love born of friendship draws breath till the moment of death.
Phocis joined Orestes and Pylades from infancy; they took a god for
witness of their mutual love, and sailed through life on a single ship.
Together they put Clytemnestra to death, as though both had been
Agamemnon's sons; by both was Aegisthus slain. Pylades suffered
even more than Orestes, when the latter was hounded by the Furies.
When Orestes was accused of being a criminal, Pylades stood by
his side. Their loving friendship was not hemmed in by the
boundaries of Greece, for they sailed together to the farthest shores
of Scythia, one ill and the other nursing him. When they reached the
land of the Tauri, the Fury herself, avenger of Orestes' mother's
murder, laid out their welcome: barbarians attacking from all sides
just as Orestes was laid low by his mad ravings. "But Pylades wiped
away the foam and tended him, covering him with a well-woven

robe,"[9] showing not so much the tenderness of a lover as that of a father. When it was decided that one would remain behind to be sacrificed while the other journeyed to Mycenae to deliver the letter, each wanted to spare the other, deeming he would live on in the one to survive. Orestes refused the letter, as if Pylades was worthier of carrying it, and was the beloved and not the lover: "If he were to die I could not bear the torment, for my ship is already overburdened with misery." And later he says: "...Give him the letter. He will go to Argos as you have wished, and as for me, let me die as you see fit."[10]

That's how things stand. When an honest love, nourished from childhood, gathers strength and reaches the manly age of reason, then the one we have long loved is able to return that love. It is hard to tell who is whose lover; just as in a mirror, the tenderness of the lover is reflected by that of the beloved. Why ever do you reproach as a lust alien to our lives that which has been decreed by divine law, and handed down from one generation to another? We have received it with joy and we cherish it as sacred treasure. Truly happy is he, as the wise have justly said, who has

> Young boys and strong-hooved horses!
> Joyfully ages the old man
> Whom youths do love.[11]

The precepts of Socrates, that admirable judge of virtue, were sanctified by the Delphic tripod. The Sybil spoke truly when she said, "Of all men, Socrates is the wisest." Besides all his other teachings benefitting the human race, he taught us that there is nothing better than the love of boys.

There is no doubt that we must love boys the same way in which Alicibiades was loved by Socrates, who slept the sleep of a father with him under a single cloak. As for me, I will end this speech with a bit of advice useful for all, taken from these verses of Callimachus:

> You who upon youths cast your longing eyes,
> The sage of Erchius[12] bids you be lovers of boys.
> Make love then to the young, the city with
> upstanding men to fill.[13]

But know this, young lovers, if you would be wise: Have dealings only with virtuous boys. Do not barter lasting devotion for a cheap thrill, else, in short order, your love will be nothing but a lie. If, however, you worship divine Eros, your beloved's sentiment will remain constant from childhood until old age. Those who love in this fashion live delightful lives. Their consciences are unstained by anything shameful, and, after death, the glory they won spreads their renown to all men. If one is to believe the sons of philosophers, the heavens themselves receive those devoted to this love, after they leave this world. They go toward a better life, there to enjoy immortality as the reward of their virtue. (*Continued on page 111*)

Hercules and Iolaus[14]

Apollo at the altar

Apollo and Hyacinthus

pollo was taking his ease in his shrine at Delphi,
surveying his lands at his leisure, alone as only a
god can be. Suddenly a stunning sight stopped
him cold: a youth, one like a god — tall, slender, a mop of
jet-black curly hair framing a gentle face, and at the peak of
beauty, too... Apollo transformed himself, took on the very
likeness of a man, and struck out for un-walled Sparta, bent
on making the boy his own. As he drew near he ran into
a musician, twanging softly on his lyre, drinking in the boy
with his eyes. Apollo made himself out to be a traveler,   *10*
foreign to those parts, and plied him with questions,
curious about them both. "They call me Thamyris the Poet,
and that's my sweetheart, Hyacinthus, son of the Spartan
king," the bard offered, unsuspecting. "That boy will be
mine," let fly Apollo, an edge to his voice. No sooner were
those words out of his mouth than Zephyrus, the West
Wind, winged down before them. He had been shadowing
the prince, and now claimed Hyacinthus for himself.

A fiery argument broke out among the three. "He's
mine! I sing to him, and, if you must know, my music puts   *20*

Zephyrus and Hyacinthus

to shame even that of the Muses!" cried Thamyris unthinking, insulting the goddesses. "Oh no, he is *mine!* I have taken him in my arms and flown him through the sky!" howled Zephyrus in anger. "What if we let the boy decide?" suggested Apollo. The three of them approached Hyacinthus and laid all before him. "Well, which one of us will you keep as lover?" they wanted to know. "Whoever is most able?" replied the youth, a bit put out, unsure whom to pick. They all began boasting of their skills at the same time, confusing him even more. In the end they agreed to hold a competition, that way a clear winner might stand out. Apollo, however, thought it wise to rid himself of

30

Thamyris blinded

Thamyris first. He did not have to lift a finger: He simply told the Muses about the poet's boast. Furious, for *they* had been the ones to inspire Thamyris all along, the goddesses rushed down and punished the poet for his pride. As his mother looked on, dumbstruck, they ripped away his voice, his sight, and all memory of music.

A great crowd gathered the next day to take in the contest, and the two remaining suitors squared off. First Zephyrus let loose with a fierce blast of wind, cold and

40

wet. It stripped the trees of leaves, and spread panic and chaos among the people. Hyacinthus was impressed. Then came Apollo's turn. He drew his silver bow and shot a shimmering arrow that spread nothing but songs and sweet pleasure in its wake. *That* won Hyacinthus over – he had never seen anything remotely like it in his life. He turned his back on the West Wind, and modestly asked Apollo to be his lover. Zephyrus stormed off in a rage, *50* swearing vengeance, but all those gathered there only smiled at his bluff and bluster.

From that day on, the two could hardly stay apart. Time and again, in Delphi, the god up and walked off, leaving his shrine untended, just to be with Hyacinthus – never had he loved anyone as much as he loved this boy. He took

Hyacinthus on the flying swan

him hunting through the scented woods and meadows, he
taught him to shoot the silver bow with sure aim. Apollo
welcomed this simple life: it wakened all his desires, and
roaming the mountain paths beside his friend fed the
fire of his love. Everything he had, Apollo put before   60
Hyacinthus; everything he did, he shared with him. When
the sun drove his chariot across the sky, the god coached
Hyacinthus in gymnastics, pouring raw strength into his
young body, and he even taught him to ride one of his
sacred swans, soaring and plunging through the sky at will,
left the boy breathless with delight. When night drew her
veil over the land, Apollo revealed to the prince the secret
ways of divination, taught him music as well, until rippling
melodies rolled easily off the boy's lyre. Hyacinthus was
filled with wonder at these awesome arts, skills undreamt   70
by man. He mastered them one by one, and passed them
on to his friends in turn, so that, thanks to him, mortals
came to learn what only the gods had known. Hyacinthus
spent all his time by Apollo's side, and his confidence grew
with every passing day.

Once, in midsummer, the lovers decided to try their
hands at throwing the discus. It was midday. The sun beat
down with blinding glare. The windless plain shimmered
in the heat. The two stripped naked, sleeked their skin
with smooth olive oil, the better to glisten in the light,   80
and stepped out into the field. Zephyrus, invisible, was
watching closely, his heart poisoned by jealousy. Apollo
gathered his might, spun, hurled the heavy metal disk.
It rose swift as a bird, cleaving the clouds in two, showing

what can be done when skill and strength are joined. Then, glittering as a star, it began to tumble down. Hyacinthus sprinted to meet it, eager to strut his stuff, his feet nimble over the rough soil. Suddenly, a gust of wind out of the west caught the discus just so. The glinting bronze glanced 90 off the ground and struck Hyacinthus sharply in the temple. The boy let out a moan and crumpled to the earth. His blood stained the grass crimson as Zephyrus flew off, taunting Apollo with cruel peals of laughter.

Apollo raced over, propped Hyacinthus up, cradled his head on his knee. He applied magic herbs, he laid on secret ointments, but still the wound refused to heal, and Apollo helplessly watched his friend slip away. Nothing worked, nothing could ever work, for not even a god's skills can undo what another god has done. There was nothing left 100 to do but curse the West Wind. Hyacinthus grew pale, his clear eyes lost their gleam. "Death is closing in on you, dear friend!" cried Apollo. "So unfair, and by my own hand too. Was it a fault to play with you, to love you? Oh, what I would give to join you! I am so sick of this endless life."

Sobbing his eyes out, Apollo held his friend close. He then bent low and whispered in his ear, "Hyacinthus, listen! You too will live forever, you'll live in my heart. When in true song I strum my lyre, your name will ring out. And you will rise again. Each spring you will rise, a 110 gorgeous flower, your name branded upon it." As he spoke, the blood upon the grass vanished. In its place a crimson blossom pushed up its head, and the god knelt and carefully inscribed an "H" at the root of each petal.

Ever since, the memory of Hyacinthus lives on among the gentlemen of Sparta. They give honors to their fallen son just as their fathers always have, and celebrate him for three whole days in midsummer, at the great Hyacinthia festival.

Discus thrower

Narcissus

Narcissus

From the moment he was born, Narcissus, son of the river god and a nymph, stood out head and shoulders above all others for his beauty. All who saw him were stunned – the infant was gorgeous – and his nurses swooned over his looks. His mother, troubled about what Fate might hold in store for such a child, took him to a seer, Tiresias by name. "Will my boy live to see old age?" the mother asked. "Yes, but only if he never knows himself," replied the diviner. No one could make any sense of his answer. 10

Narcissus was sixteen now, and his beauty blazed full force. All the men and women in town melted for him, yet he shunned every last one, and kept his beauty to himself. His neighbor, Ameinias, loved him more than all the others put together. Day in, day out, he saw Narcissus pass his house, and simply could not keep his eyes off the radiant youth. The boy, of course, paid him scant notice. Finally, out of his wits with longing, Ameinias waylaid Narcissus. He bared his heart, begged him to be his beloved. Narcissus held his tongue. A sharpened dagger, 20

sent with a slave, was his answer. Ameinias caught on.
He stood on Narcissus' doorstep, lifted his hands to the
skies, called down the wrath of the gods upon the one who
spurned him: "Let him, too, be consumed by love …and
let him be denied the one he craves!" Then he turned the
dagger on himself. Narcissus was unmoved. Just as before,
he turned a cold shoulder to anyone caught in the web of
his beauty. But Artemis, the cruel goddess of the hunt, had
heard Ameinias' plea and made sure to fulfill it.

30   One day, Narcissus went up into the mountains on a
hunting expedition. He set out his fine-woven nets and
bushwhacked through the woods, hoping to flush out some
majestic stag, to drive it into his trap. His mind all on the
hunt, Narcissus lost track of time, lost his way as well, and
roamed ever deeper into the ancient forest. When he finally
stopped and looked around, he had no idea where he
found himself – it was a place he had never seen before.
Worn out with walking, he kneeled by a cool spring, clear
as crystal. He bent down to drink, but as one thirst was
40   quenched a greater one sprang up in him: staring open-
eyed from the limpid pool was the most gorgeous guy
he had ever seen.

Narcissus caught his breath, his eyes thirstily roving over
the boy's every trait – the shock of curly blond hair, the
smooth flushed cheek, the chest, rippling with muscles, and
what a dish he was! Narcissus bent down to plant a tender
kiss on him, but only cold water met his lips. He grasped
at his hand, but his fingers brought up only tangled weeds.
He turned to the mute trees: "Has any lover met such

96

Goddess of Revenge

50 scorn? Has a beloved ever been so close, and yet so far? I
see him, he sees me. I smile at him, he smiles back. I reach
for him, and his fingers rise to meet mine. I bend to kiss
him and he offers me his mouth. He is keen to be held,
and yet ... Enough, already! Come, let's hold each other
tight! Why do you toy with me? I am neither old nor ugly.
In fact, plenty of people come on to me, too. Or, could it
be ... ? Yes, *that* must be it! You are none other than myself,
aren't you? What cruel longing is this, that longs for that
which never left, and turns wealth to poverty?"

60   Narcissus felt his life force drain away. His passion, in
exchange, grew stronger than ever, a raving madness now.
"Why do you leave me? Don't go!" he insisted. "Why so
cruel? At least let my eyes feast upon what my body cannot
have." Certain his love was forever out of reach, he tore his
hair and clawed his face and chest. Then he bent down
again to look, and the boy he loved stared back at him, all
ragged and disheveled now. Seeing the other's pain broke
his heart, and he sobbed helplessly. "I love you! I love you!"
he shouted again and again into the water.

70   There was no way he could tear himself away from his
beloved, Narcissus realized. He sank down upon the grass,
there by the edge of the spring, and took his life with his
sword, his face a mask of pain. His soul flitted down to
Hades, to the banks of the river Styx, and there he keeps
on bending down to look at himself in its dark waters. On
Earth, the nymphs of the spring found his corpse, and saw
he had once been beautiful. They left it by the waterside
and went off to build a pyre and ready torches for a proper

funeral. But when they returned to bear the body off, it
was nowhere to be found. Where he had lain, a new flower   *80*
bloomed, its golden petals fringed with white, its head
dipping down towards the water. An intoxicating perfume
wafted from it, and to this day its essence numbs the body
and the mind.

Narcissus at the spring

Achilles and Patroclus

Achilles and Patroclus

The war to end all wars was in the making: All Europe was rising up against all Asia to right a wrong that cried out for revenge. Paris, prince of Troy, an honored guest in Menelaus' royal halls, had stolen Helen, his host's splendid wife, raided his treasure house in dark of night, then hightailed it back to the safety of his father's city to enjoy his loot and captive to the hilt. The Greeks, to a man, rose up in anger and readied for war, vowing to level the looming walls of Troy and free Helen. Mountains were stripped of trees for lumber to build fast ships; fields were emptied of farmers to fill the rank and file of the army; treasuries of ruddy bronze and gold and grey iron were beaten into swords and armor. No man was left behind, no man shirked gory battle, lest he be stripped of all his wealth. The Greeks sailed their beaked ships to Troy, beached them close by, flung up a great barricade to keep them safe, and laid siege to the city.

    Ten years passed and still the Greeks had not breached the black walls of Troy with their crown of towers. The neighboring towns, though, fell one by one. Noble Achilles,

10

20

the fiercest of the Greek fighters, led the troops headlong
into battle, like some savage beast unleashed, and his dear
friend, Patroclus, fought always by his side, tempering
Achilles' wildness and pride with loving sound advice. The
Greeks laid waste to all the land, plundered its wealth, its
women. Agamemnon, their general, then parceled out the
spoils, and the loveliest girl, Briseis, fell to Achilles' lot.

Rampaging through the towns like men possessed, the
Greeks even outraged the boys. Achilles himself ripped
30 out the life of lord Apollo's own dear son, the handsome
Troilus, cut off his head on the god's very altar because
the boy refused his caresses. In Troy, however, the fury of
the Greeks merely pent up the Trojans, under Hector's
command, inside the impregnable citadel. But now
thundering Zeus turned his face from the Greeks, and
smiled instead upon the Trojans. They poured out the city
gates, pushed the Greek armies hard against their ships,
shattered their defenses. The Greeks fought for their lives,
tears running down their cheeks for the wives and children
40 they would not see again, looking right, looking left, no
one there to save them now.

All that because one warrior chief had turned his back
on the pitched battle – Achilles himself. He refused to fight,
and kept his men holed up in their ships. His warriors, with
Patroclus foremost, clamored to disembark and join the fray,
but Achilles would not hear of it. He raged, Achilles did,
against Agamemnon. He had reached unbidden into
Achilles' tent, had snatched his hard-earned plunder, his
darling Briseis, before the eyes of all the Greeks, in a fit of

Achilles and Briseis

fury at losing his own slave. There and then Achilles swore   50
he would fight no more for that shameless Agamemnon, not
until the slaughter broke against his own ships. The Greeks
would turn to him in their hour of need, and call to him in
vain, and then they would be sorry, who witnessed his
disgrace and just stood by.

  Now, as Hector and his men mauled the Greeks without
mercy, that hour had come. Now Agamemnon bitterly rued
his madness. He gnashed his teeth and cried tears of blood
to see his friends cut down, no help in sight. Twice he had
sent urgent envoys, his fellow nobles, the men Achilles   60
loved the best, to beg his help with promises of gold and

Achilles and Chiron

women – even Briseis herself, and Agamemnon had not yet bedded her. Twice Achilles sent them away empty-handed. They could go to their death, for all he cared. Finally, Patroclus, heartbroken to see his friends fight to the last man beside the long black ships, could bear it no longer. He went weeping to Achilles, but before he could utter a word, his friend called out, "Why these girl's tears, Patroclus?

Not for the Greeks, paying for their sins, I hope!" "You
heart of iron, unreasonable man!" answered Patroclus, "If   70
you are afraid of some secret doom, at least send *me* into
battle, let our army follow my command and lend me your
god-forged armor. The Trojans might mistake me for you,
might flee headlong back to walled Troy. Even now they are
setting fire to our ships." Achilles could not refuse Patroclus,
he loved the man too much. He lent him the divine armor,
under strict orders only to drive the Trojans from the ships
and then return at once, lest some god rise up against him.

Alone again, Achilles prayed to Zeus, soaking the earth
with wine, begged him to grant his friend success and safe   80
return. His prayer came straight from the heart, for Patroclus
was his one true love. At gatherings they always sat apart
from the crowd, arms around each other, laying their plans,
and when all turned in, the two shared a single blanket.
Achilles had no use for any of the Greeks, and wished he
and Patroclus alone could take on all of Troy. So it had been
ever since Achilles' father had sent them, still raw youths, to
live with that wise centaur Chiron in his mountain cave, to
learn to hunt and fight, and to remain innocent of men's evil
ways. Under Chiron's eye Achilles grew to wield spear and   90
sword better than any man alive. Patroclus strove hard to
match his feats, but Achilles, though younger, was stronger
by far. Facing their trials side by side, the boys grew close
and went from love to greater love.

Fresh to the fight, thirsty for slaughter, Patroclus and his
troops turned the tide of battle, thrust back the worn out
Trojans from the burning ships, put out the fires. Giddy

with success they pressed on, farther and farther to the black walls of Troy itself. Routed, the Trojans drew back, and back again, struggling for dear life. Many fell under Patroclus' lance that day, so many that Apollo himself took notice and stepped in to help his favored troops. One blow from him, and Achilles' golden armor went flying into the dust. Stunned, Patroclus did not see coming the lance that struck between his shoulder blades, nor the one Hector thrust through the gut. Patroclus fell to the earth and clawed the bloody dust, the name of Achilles on his lips.

Horror gripped the Greeks, to see sweet life ripped from Patroclus. Too late to save him, they fought like lions to claim his body and his armor but Hector overpowered them all, and no one could brave him now. He grabbed the god-forged armor for himself, and would have taken Patroclus' head as well, but the Greeks managed to drive him back, and bore away the broken corpse to Achilles' lodge. Black grief crushed Achilles, his eyes brimmed with endless tears. He threw himself upon Patroclus' body, full of reproaches for throwing his life away: "Why so ungrateful, after all our kisses? Why so uncaring for the holy union of our thighs?" He mourned without let, forgetting sleep, forgetting food and drink, and day after day put off the funeral, unable to part with his friend.

Even the goddess Thetis, Achilles' mother, resting on the bottom of the sea, heard his cries and hurried to his side. "My child, how long will you go on mourning like this? It is a good thing to lie in love with a woman, too!" But even as life left Patroclus, so the will to live left Achilles.

Thetis with new armor

Now his only wish was to destroy the man who had killed
his friend, though he knew full well his own death must
follow Hector's, for Fate commanded it. Thetis brought
him new armor, again forged by a god. Heedless of certain   130
doom, Achilles donned his new gear and raced to battle.
With cold, relentless fury he chased down Hector and tore
out his life, dragged his body round and round walled Troy
and off to his own lodge as an offering to dead Patroclus.

That night, however, his friend's ghost came to him in a dream: "You cared well for me in life, Achilles, but not in death. Bury me quickly, for your fate awaits you. And one more request, grant it please: Do not place my bones apart from yours, let them lie together in a single urn, as

140   we grew up in your father's house." "Why tell me what I already know? I'll do it all," answered Achilles, "but, oh, come closer, let's throw our arms about each other, just for one moment..." Achilles reached out, but Patroclus slipped through his fingers like fog, and he sprang awake in the empty room.

    "Hard on the heels of Hector's death, your own must come at once," Achilles' own mother had warned him. He had always gone fearless into battle, for he knew Thetis had held him by his heel and dipped him, still an infant, in the

150   dark waters of the Styx, had made his skin invulnerable to weapons. Now, however, he waited for death, and wondered how it would get the better of him. The Trojans, too, were sunk in gloom. Hector, their best man by far, was dead, and they thirsted for revenge. Paris, his brother, seized his bow, took command with winging words, called out firm orders. The gates of Troy again flung open, again the hordes of fighters poured out onto the dusty plain. The Greeks too rose as one man, and the wild joy of war gripped Achilles. He plowed, unstoppable, through the

160   enemy host, and the hearts of the Trojan heroes broke to see their companions writhing in the dust. Achilles reached the city's very gates, but there Apollo stopped him cold. Long had the god thirsted for his beloved Troilus' blood

price. With sure hand he guided Paris' arrow: The polished shaft flew true, its sharp bronze dug into Achilles' heel, the only spot untouched by Stygian waters. Waves of agony washed over Achilles. His life left him and his shade flew straight to the White Island in the Black Sea, the wooded island filled with game at the mouth of the Danube river. There it joined the roaming soul of Patroclus, and they *170* while away the time hunting and feasting arm in arm, the two of them and many other heroes, honored to this day with holy sacrifices by the tribesmen along that wild coast.

Pan teaching Daphnis

Different Loves

Lycinus concludes his account of Callicratidas' speech, and reveals his choice of winner.

Part IV

LYCINUS: *(Quoting Callicratidas)* If one is to believe the sons of philosophers, the heavens themselves receive those devoted to this love, after they leave this world. They go toward a better life, there to enjoy immortality as the reward of their virtue.

After Callicratidas' speech, solemn, yet brimming with youthful elan, I stopped Charicles, who was about to reply, and pointed out that it was time for us to go down to the ship. Both my companions, however, pressed me to pass judgement. I reflected briefly on their speeches, and said, "You do not seem, my friends, to have spoken idly or thoughtlessly. By Zeus, your words give proof of deep and lengthy consideration. You hardly left anything for another to use of what needs be said on this topic, and your eloquence matched your erudition; I wish I were Theramenes the Buskin[1], so you could remain on equal footing, winners both. But because you will not spare me, and also because I wish the rest of our trip not to be troubled by such arguments, I will tell you what, at this point, seems most fair.

"Marriage is a useful thing for men, and a happy one, if a good match is made. But I believe that boyish loves, to the extent they obey the chaste laws of friendship, are the only ones worthy of philosophy. Therefore all should be compelled to marry, but let only philosophers be permitted the love of boys. In truth, virtue does not reach perfection among women. So do not be angry, Charicles, if Corinth yields to Athens."

Having pronounced this verdict in spare and restrained words I rose to my feet. Charicles hung his head like one sentenced to death. But the Athenian, his brow held high, stepped forward joyfully. He looked as if he just had singlehandedly defeated the Persians at

Salamis. I received from him a further reward for my decision, for he invited us to a splendid triumphal feast, one in keeping with his generous lifestyle. I quietly comforted Charicles, praising his eloquence, even more admirable for having defended the weaker cause.

Thus ended our stay in Cnidus and our conversation by the temple of the goddess, where we mixed playfulness with culture. But you, Theomnestus, who evoked these old remembrances of mine, how would you have decided, had you been judge?

THEOMNESTUS: By the gods, do you take me for a fool like Melitides or Coroebus,[2] to render an opinion contrary to yours? Your delightful tale made me feel as if I had been with you in Cnidus myself, and I almost took this little dwelling to be the temple of Aphrodite. Nevertheless, as one may say anything on a holiday, and the fun, even if heavyhanded, is part of it, I was somewhat taken aback by the pompous bombast of the speech on male love. In fact, it seems hardly pleasant to pass all your days in the company of a boy already past puberty, bearing the torments of Tantalus as you suffer from thirst, his beauty bathing your eyes, yet remaining impossible to drink. It is not enough merely to see the one you love, to remain seated before him, nor just to listen to him talk. Pleasure for Eros is like a ladder: Sight is the first step, but as soon as he has seen, he desires to get closer and to touch; and as soon as he has touched with his fingertips, enjoyment courses through his whole body. When the occasion presents itself, he risks, thirdly, a discreet kiss, lips gently touching lips. Hardly have they met when he draws back, to quell suspicion. Taking advantage of new opportunities, he indulges in longer embraces. His mouth draws back time and again, but his hands must not remain still – daring caresses through the clothes excite desire. Or perhaps he will gently slide his furtive right hand into the bosom, to press nipples that swell a bit more than usual; he then slowly explores the whole expanse of a firm stomach, then the flower of puberty in its early down. "But why must I speak of secret things?"[3] Finally, Eros, having attained the power, goes about a hotter business and, leaping from the thighs, as the comic poet says, "strikes where he must."[4]

That, in my opinion, is how one should love boys. Let these inspired windbags, and all who aspire to highbrow philosophy, nourish the ignorant with the ringing sound of honest words. Socrates was a true lover, if ever there was one, and Alcibiades, who lay down under the same tunic with him, did not get up unstruck. Don't be surprised: Patroclus in fact, was not loved by Achilles just because he was seated before him, "waiting for Achilles to finish his song."[5] It was lust that mediated their friendship. Achilles, moaning upon the death of Patroclus, lets his unchecked passion burst out with the power of truth when he says, "My tears mourn the holy union of our thighs."[6]

And, by the way, it seems to me those dubbed "revelers"[7] by the Greeks are nothing but professional lovers. Some might call this a shameful thing to say, but at least it is the truth, by Aphrodite of Cnidus!

LYCINUS: I will not let you, dear Theomnestus, launch into a third speech just as this holiday is drawing to a close. I would only hear the beginning, the rest never to reach my ears. Come, let us not tarry any further, but head for the marketplace: the pyre of Hercules is about to be put to the torch. The show is not devoid of interest, and brings to mind his sufferings on Oeta.[8]

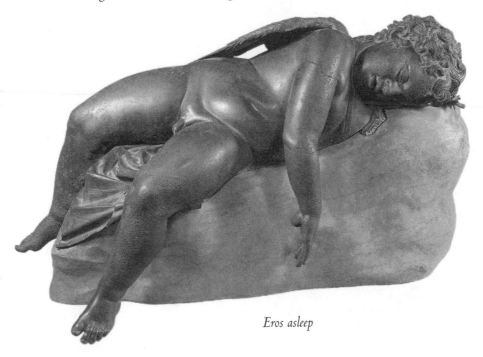

Eros asleep

Aphrodite

Afterword

First, as it seems, we must supervise the makers of tales; and if they make a fine tale, it must be approved, but if it's not, it must be rejected. We'll persuade nurses and mothers to tell the approved tales to their children and to shape their souls with tales more than their bodies with hands. Many of those they now tell must be thrown out.

— Plato, *The Republic*[1]

A comparison of any modern book of mythology or legend with the original sources will show clearly how well the world has heeded Socrates' advice that mythical and legendary tales should be censored before they are told to young people. At a time when young adult novelists, refreshingly, have acknowledged their readers' interest in matters of romance and sexuality, high school and college students who are introduced to mythology continue to be offered tales that have been fig-leafed as effectively as Victorian statues.

Take, for example, this adaptation of the tale of what happened when sixteen-year-old Narcissus saw his own reflection in a pool of water:

> He blinked his eyes and looked again. It was still there — the most beautiful face he had ever seen. As beautiful, he knew, as his own, but with a nimbus of light behind it so that the hair was blurred and looked long — like a girl's. He gazed and gazed and could not have enough of it. He knew that he could look upon this face forever and still not be satisfied. He put out his hand to touch her.[2]

No one would guess, while reading this version of the tale, that in the original story Narcissus fell in love with the image of a beautiful young man.

The above adaptation at least retains the love interest, but other renditions of Greek mythology seek to hide even that. The tragedy of this distortion of the original tales is not confined to the damage it creates to accurate historical knowledge. While the debate in this book reminds readers that sexual love between males has always been a matter for dispute, readers who disapprove of such love ought not to applaud the purging of such stories. Modern readers, whatever their views on homosexuality, should mourn the loss of a tradition that could assist them in a struggle that many people today are undertaking: to comprehend the sacred aspects of sexual love.

For people living in the West, this is a hard task. Plato's belief that the body and spirit are always at war with each other, combined with similar views arriving from the Middle East, has had two effects on Western spirituality. One has been a heightened awareness of the dangerous aspects of sexuality, resulting in a vigorous defense against its darker side. The other, less fortunate, result has been that Westerners often regard sexuality as the enemy of divinity.

Westerners who wish to learn and teach about the spiritual benefits of sexuality are therefore faced with an uphill battle. A few passing references in the Bible, occasional hints of romantic love between the saints, obscure and disputed references in non-canonical literature, religious poems from a much later period – these are the foundations of recent attempts to break away from the extreme asceticism of the late classical and medieval periods and establish a more balanced spirituality of sexual love. Unfortunately, many of the West's major sacred texts were formulated during late antiquity and the early Middle Ages, when otherworldliness was at its height. One can judge the nature of that period by recalling that the hot debate among early Christian writers was not whether homosexuality was immoral, but whether *marriage* was immoral. However great the benefits are of an ascetic worldview, such a perspective is necessarily imbalanced, and Western faiths are often deficient in texts that promote a view of sexual love as a priceless road to the divine.

Even Western paganism turned its face from sacred sexuality in late antiquity, and if the pagan faiths had continued past the fall of the Roman Empire, it is quite possible that their modern versions would have been as sex-negative as other Western faiths have been throughout much of their history. The classical myths, though, come from an earlier period, when the dark elements of sexuality were recognized, but the link between sexuality and spirituality had not yet been severed by Plato's over enthusiastic followers.

Precisely because these stories come from an earlier period, it may be hard for modern readers to take their spiritual message seriously. Gods who abduct and rape the young men they love? What sort of spirituality is that? Yet it should be remembered that these stories were created during the same time period as the Old Testament God, who demanded that the Jews rape captive women. By the time that rabbinic Judaism and early Christianity developed a higher ethic, a more refined paganism was also developing, wary of the immorality of the earlier gods. These later gods, though, were less interested in love.

The talent of Andrew Calimach is that he has managed to recreate the earlier stories in a manner that helps us to understand the intimate connection the Greeks saw between falling in love and revering the gods. The reader need not go far in this volume before a different and long abandoned world bursts into view: A world in which the gods place their lovers among the stars.

Calimach's rendition of the tales is in no way prurient; the stories have a softer, romantic touch to them. Yet the stories succeed in showing us the deep emotions the Greek men and their gods felt toward the youths they courted. Whether the narratives tell of Orpheus singing of his love as death approaches, Achilles mourning the loss of Patroclus' kisses, tear-stained Apollo cursing his own immortality and pleading to join his dead beloved in Hades, or Laius lamely excusing his rape of a youth by saying, "I know what I am doing, but nature forces me," Calimach's adaptations are filled with pathos and beauty that bear comparison with the original tales.

"If there was some necessity to tell" the forbidden tales of the gods, Socrates said in *The Republic*, "as few as possible ought to hear them as unspeakable secrets, after making a sacrifice, not of a pig but of some great offering that's hard to come by, so that it will come to the ears of the smallest possible number." Fortunately, this book ensures that such love stories will reach the ears of a wider audience than has hitherto been privileged to hear the true myths and legends of the world.

Heather Elizabeth Peterson
March 2000

Storyteller's Postscript

Ever since I first got wind of these myths, I wanted to read them in full, to savor their rich flavor. But whenever I reached out for this or that compilation, I was disappointed to find scant, if any, mention of male love. Finally, I decided to gather the stories myself, despite being unfamiliar with the classics, an experience a lot like that of "a blind man finding a jewel in a heap of dust." I can only hope that my amateur effort will inspire someone better qualified to do justice to these important and beautiful myths, cornerstones of the gay canon.

Most of the homoerotic Greek myths exist as fragments, occasionally conflicting ones, scattered throughout surviving ancient texts. Reassembling them has been much like putting an ancient vase back together. First the pieces had to be dug up, then checked for fit. Time and again the shards seemed to take on a life of their own, arranging themselves in unexpected ways. Often, gaps remained. At times the missing piece turned up after a bit more digging, else plaster had to be shaped to plug the hole. I would like to think the makers of the vases, upon seeing the restorations, would claim them as their own.

Along the way I began to realize how much Greek mythology, in its current incarnations, has been altered in deference to modern sensibilities. This process has intensified in recent years, as myth and folklore have been co-opted by mass market commercial interests beholden to the imperative to appeal to all and offend none. In the process, the rough primal beauty and terrible symmetry of Greek myth have inevitably been diluted. When we understand Oedipus' sufferings stem from his father's rape of a boy, they take on deeper meaning. Likewise, Aphrodite's birth rings truer to the poetic ear when we learn she arose from the spilled seed of Uranus,[1] rather than from mere sea water. These and many other hidden gems bring Greek myth to vivid life, illuminating the ancient world view as well as the modern mind.

Aphrodite

We, the parents of today, are not the only ones shortchanged. Our young have been cheated as well, by being handed a pantheon of emasculated gods and heroes. Myth, at once primitive and sophisticated, is a pedagogy as well as a psychology. It communicates enduring human values, and speaks to people of all ages. The watering down of myth saps its power to resonate with the mind, to teach its lessons of honor, duty, love, courage, humility, wisdom, and the sanctity of all experience. One can only wonder whether these once-sacred stories might be even more popular in their authentic forms, and whether, by discovering in them the full spectrum of desire, our children might grow up more tolerant of each other, and richer in self-esteem and self-acceptance.

My only regret is that there is nothing here about the love of women for one another. Their history has been even more thoroughly effaced than that of male love[2], because their oppressors were usually as close as the same bed, or the next room, and always the ones in power.[3]

For those of us who have grown up with the conventional view of myth and history, these stories may be nothing short of mind-altering, forcing a re-evaluation of our ancestors, lovingly outed in these pages. Would it be too much to hope for a re-evaluation of ourselves as well, and of our conventional Western pigeonholing of erotic experience?

Andrew Calimach
Tantallon, Nova Scotia
August 2001

Acknowledgments

This book is in your hands thanks mainly to the pioneering work of scholars who overcame many obstacles, often at significant professional risk, to bring to light the history of male love. They are too numerous to mention here, but the merit for making this material available is largely theirs.

The credit for whatever dramatic power these stories might have must go to Agi Lev, the theater director who struggled through reams of plodding prose to resurrect the living essence of each story and make it rise from the page.

Heather Elizabeth Peterson made me think I could write, the vital push that got the ball rolling. Dr. Thomas Carpenter helped resolve problems relating to Greek iconography, and was patient enough to debate unorthodox interpretations of Greek myth. Giovanni Dall'Orto pointed out key examples of Etruscan and Roman art. Jeff Grygny conceived and executed the Greek map, a true delight! Bea Ferrigno, my editor, turned a rough draft into a finished work — her experience helped make up for my lack of it. M. Ishino turned her titanic organizational skills to bibliographical details. The indefatigable Lorenzo Smerillo was an invaluable help with Greek and Latin translations. Carolyn Ross kindly put to use her knowledge of librarian lore in finding rare texts. Ken Wallace has been a stalwart; the thanks for laying out this visual feast go to him.

Many museums and institutions both in Europe and in the United States put their resources at my disposal, often at no cost. A couple stand out. In the US, the staff at the The Getty were unusually kind and helpful. In Europe, the staff at the British Museum went out of their way time and again to help me with the illustrations — hospitably granting me access to their reserve collection and doing their utmost to supply me with all the needed reproductions; Dr. Alfred Bernhard-Walcher at the Vienna Kunsthistorisches Museum assisted me greatly with my research; Dr F. W. Hamdorf, at the Staatliche Antikensammlungen Museum in Munchen, generously and unassumingly lent his help. Dr. Alessandra Villone, at the Soprintendenza Archeologica di Napoli e Caserta, spared no effort in finding essential materials.

My lovers, children, and friends have been more than kind and tolerant with my arcane interests; the good karma they have accumulated is inexhaustible.

A final thanks to the many others who gave of themselves to see this project reach fruition, but who, due to the somewhat provocative nature of this work, prefer to remain anonymous. I can only hope that, as a result of their efforts, people someday will no longer have anything to fear when talking about love.

Notes & Sources

BELOVED CHARIOTEERS

1 Straton of Sardis, *Musa Paidike* (The Boyish Muse), in *The Greek Anthology*, Cambridge: Harvard University Press, Loeb Classical Library, 1918, XII #228 (Author's rendition)

2 Plato, *Symposium,*, Tom Griffith, Tr. Berkeley: University of California Press, 1986, 181d

3 B. Sergent, *Homosexuality in Greek Myth*, A. Goldhammer, Tr. Boston: Beacon Press, 1986, 40.

4 The artistic convention for scenes of seduction was to show the lover fondling the young man's genitals with one hand, and with the other cupping his chin to look him in the eye. Youths were shown putting up various degrees of resistance, as it was not cool to give in without a fight. In this case the young man is presenting only token resistance, for he is not preventing anything. Two other men, one holding a sacrificial fawn, dance delightedly.

5 Or, in Greek, *eromenos* for "beloved" and *erastes* for "lover."

6 In Greek poetry, there seems to be a regular homoerotic connection between the chariot rider (the senior fighter and the chariot's owner) and the chariot driver (the younger male, often coming of age, clearly the less-experienced fighter).

7 The Spartan terms are evocative: The youth was the *aïtas*, or "hearer," and his lover, the *eispnelas*, or "inspirer."

8 Xenophon, Symposium VIII, and The Lacedemonian Republic, II, in R. Peyrefitte, *La Muse Garçonniere*, Paris: Flammarion, 1973, 150.

9 Callimachus, *Aetia, Iambi, Hecale and Other Fragments*, C. A. Trypanis, Tr. Cambridge: Harvard University Press, Loeb Classical Library, 1958, 571.

10 See Lucian's *Different Loves*, Part II, p. 37 in this volume.

11 In Petronius' *Satyricon*, Quartilla, a temple prostitute, quotes this proverb (Posse taurum tollere, qui vitulum sustulerit) to illustrate how the age of her lovers has kept pace with her own. Its use there, of course, makes little sense, as grown women need no justification for making love to adult men. Furthermore, the proverb is shot through with masculine imagery. Thus, coming from Quartilla in that context, it reads as a hilarious malapropism – Petronius' ironical aside on the love of adult men for others of their own kind, and on their self-justification in the face of societal disapproval. This reading is all the more plausible as the *Satyricon* has the love of youths as its central theme. Petronius Arbiter, *The Satyricon*, III.67

The saying is believed to have originally sprung from the story of Milo of Croton, thought to have lived around 500 BCE. He was said to have trained for weight-lifting by carrying a young calf on his shoulders every day from its birth until it grew to full size four years later. Then he butchered it and ate it. Quintilian, *Institutio Oratoria*, I.9; Aelian, *Varia Historia*, xii.22.

12 "Greece" was not a homogeneous nation. Local culture, language, laws, and tradition varied enormously from city to city. The area encompassed by the Greek world stretched from what is now Albania to the major islands in the Aegean Sea, North Africa, and coastal Turkey, as well as Italy and its islands. Greek culture spanned more than 2000 years. The Greeks themselves considered each region a country in its own right, and each citizen identified with, and was loyal to, his state rather than to the whole Hellenic domain. So, necessarily, what we will say about the Greeks will often be true of some areas and periods and not of others.

13 Such as Admetus, Hymenaeus, Phorbas the Lapith, and Hippolytus. Sergent, *Hom.* 262 – 263.

14 This is a controversial interpretation of the myth of Kaineus, a story in which Kainis, a nymph, is loved by Poseidon. When the god encourages her to name a love-gift, she asks to become an invincible man. Ostensibly this is not a story about male love, but it has many parallels with the story of Achilles, who also "was a woman" in his youth, and with the story of Pelops, also loved by Poseidon and given manly gifts. Thus the myth calls to mind the "standard model" of pederastic initiation. Sergent, *Hom.* 247– 249.

15 Sophocles, *The Colchian Woman* [after Athenaeus, 602]

16 These last two stories, however, appear later, and may have been literary inventions. Sergent, *Hom.* 259–260.

17 One of his mysteries *has* survived to this day, thanks largely to the imprecations of Clement of Alexandria, an early Christian preacher, who tried to hold up to ridicule the secrets of the pagans. (Pausanias also mentions the existence of this rite, but being himself a pagan, does not divulge the details). This is how the story goes:

Semele, Dionysus' mother, ended up in Hades. Jealous Hera had tricked her, while Semele was heavy with Zeus' child, into asking her lover to show himself in his true form. Bound to grant her one wish, Zeus came to her bearing his bolts of lightning, despite his better judgement. Semele and her palace were burned to cinders. The god, however, managed to save his unborn child, Dionysus.

When Dionysus came of age he made up his mind to bring his mother back to the world of the living. However, he did not know the way to Hades. A man named Prosymnus offered to direct him, but in exchange for a favor: the love of Dionysus himself. The god willingly heard the request, and swore a sacred oath to fulfil it, if only Prosymnus would wait until he returned from the underworld. Prosymnus agreed to the deal, and showed him the way.

After rescuing Semele, Dionysus remembered his promise and returned to Lerna, only to learn Prosymnus had died. The god went to Prosymnus' tomb, cut a fig branch, carved it to resemble the male member, and sat on it in order to satisfy Prosymnus' shade. Thus he fulfilled his promise to his lover and consummated their love bond. Ever after, in the various cities of Lerna, phalli were dedicated to Dionysus as mystic memorials to this deed. Clement of Alexandria, *Protrepticus* II, 34.3-5; Pausanias, *Descriptions of Greece* II, 37.5.

18 Theocritus, *Idyll 13*, in *Greek Bucolic Poets,* J. M. Edmonds, Tr. Cambridge: Harvard University Press, Loeb Classical Library, 1912

19 His love for Hylas is explored in this work. About the "lesser beloveds" we know almost nothing beyond a few of their names, such as Abderus, Philoctetes, Euphemus, and Elacatas, some of the better known ones. Sergent, *Hom.* 161-166.

20 The love between Hercules and Iolaus is discussed in the notes to "Hercules and Hylas", page 137.

21 Of the other heroes, Agamemnon, the general of Trojan war fame, fell in love with the divinely beautiful Argynnus, whom he surprised swimming naked in the river Cephissus. The poet Thamyris fell for Hymaeneus, presumably before meeting his other great flame, Hyacinthus. Philolaus the Corinthian, who gave laws to the Thebans, loved Diocles, the Olympic victor. They remained together to the end of their days. Their twin tombs were famous in the ancient world: Lovers traveled there to swear faith to each other. Cleomachus, too, had a beloved, before whom he gave his life in battle. Timagoras was head over heels in love with the ungrateful Meles, which proved his undoing, driving him to throw himself off a cliff to prove his devotion. The legendary Cretan king Minos had several beloveds, his charioteer among them, and Theseus the Athenian may also have been one. Likewise, there are indications that Phaeton, the foolhardy son of the sun, and Cycnus may have been an item. After Phaeton fell from the sky, Cycnus dove time and again for his body, and finally was turned into a swan, though another story makes him the beloved of Phylius. The Trojans are represented here by Paris, Helen's ravisher, and by Deiphobus, one of their strongest fighters. They both loved the same youth, Antheus by name (not the same one as Hermes' beloved). Finally, the mythic couple Orestes and Pylades were thought by some in ancient times to have been lovers, though others argued against that claim, just as Achilles and his best friend Patroclus were a subject of contention (see story), as were any couples who did not fit the Greek model of age-structured relationships. Sergent, *Hom.*, passim.

DIFFERENT LOVES - PART I

1   The origins of male love are lost in the mists of prehistory. In fact, they go back to the dawn of man, if observations of animals in the wild are any guide. Though same-sex sexual activity is widespread throughout the animal kingdom, it is predominantly a characteristic of higher species: The more evolved the animal the more frequent its occurrence. (See Bruce Bagemihl, *Biological Exuberance: Animal Homosexuality and Natural Diversity*, New York, St. Martin's Press, 1999)

    We have no way of knowing what animals think of this topic. Humans, however, are possessed of speech, so that wherever a history of male love has survived, so have records of the disputes surrounding it. This debate has been going on, in various forms, for over two thousand years, so it is unlikely to be concluded any time soon. We might, however, steal a page from the arguments of our forefathers, and inject a little humor and poetry into our modern-day debates. Perhaps then the chase for some absolute truth will not be so all-consuming.

    This dialogue was written in Greek in the early years of our era by someone claiming to be Lucian of Samosata (a town on the Euphrates), but believed by many scholars to be an impostor, judging by its style. It reveals to our twenty-first-century eyes prejudice and petulant misogyny as well as humor; a sense of play, sometimes fair and sometimes not; and a seriousness leavened by lightness of heart. Before us are arrayed the trappings of philosophical inquiry, along with spurious arguments presented with great vehemence. We would be justified to conclude that many things have not changed in the past two thousand years, while we smile at how much has, indeed, changed.

2   The heads of the Hydra, denizen of the Lernean marsh; when one was cut, two more sprang from the stump.

3   Helios, who saw all from his chariot in the sky, spied Aphrodite in Ares' arms. He wasted no time in telling her husband, Hephaistos, the god of blacksmiths. He fashioned an unbreakable net, trapped the entwined lovers in the act, and displayed them to the other gods. Aphrodite never forgave Helios, and paid back his treachery by persecuting his mortal daughters.

4 The women of Lemnos had no respect for Aphrodite. As punishment, the goddess cursed them with a stench so foul, it drove their men away.

5 Hippolytus, the son of Theseus, hated women, and so remained chaste. Aphrodite took mortal offense, and caused his stepmother to fall in love with him. He rejected her too, and she, afraid he might reveal her advances, denounced him to her husband for assault. Theseus believed her, and had his father, Poseidon, kill Hippolytus.

6 The three daughters of Lycambes were publicly (and falsely) accused, by a spurned suitor, of "being easy" and luring men with their wiles, upon which they hung themselves for shame.

TANTALUS AND THE OLYMPIANS

7th c. BCE   Homer *Odyssey*, 11.567
476 BCE   Pindar *Olympian Odes*, I
408 BCE   Euripides *Orestes*, 12-16
140 BCE   Apollodorus *Epitomes* 2: 1-9
8 CE   Ovid *Metamorphoses*, VI: 213, 458
1st c. CE   Hyginus *Fables*, 82: Tantalus; 83: Pelops
160–176 CE   Pausanias *Description of Greece*, 2.22.3

LINE 43: It appears that by Classical times the shamanic dimensions of this myth were forgotten. Pindar, the oldest source of information about the feast, recoils (or claims to) at the thought of the gods "gorging" on human flesh.

LINE 55: The role of Demeter, the principal deity of the Eleusinian mysteries *and* the presiding deity at Tantalus' feast, as well as her significance in a shamanic myth in which the father is given Promethean dimensions for his theft of "the food of the gods," and the son undergoes mystical death and transfiguration, attaining (temporary!) immortality, has ramifications too complex to explore here.

LINE 77: Pelops' epithets underline his claim to fame: "the mighty charioteer," "the Phrygian Charioteer," etc.

LINE 86: The standard version of the tale, in which Tantalus is punished for "trying to fool the gods" seems to be an interpretation lent the story in later days, when the "cannibalism" of the story was no longer understood in its original, shamanic and symbolic context. Once the sacrifice of the boy was interpreted literally, the deed had to be punished. The present version is intended to be more consistent with the apparent original thrust of the tale.

PELOPS IN PISA

476 BCE	Pindar *Olympian Ode*, I
430–415 BCE	Sophocles (1) *Electra*, 504
408 BCE	Sophocles (2) *Oinomaus*, Fr. 433
408 BCE	Euripides *Orestes*, 1024-1062
140 BCE	Apollodorus *Epitomes* 2, 1-9
1st c. BCE	Diodorus Siculus *Histories*, 4.73.
1st c. CE	Hyginus *Fables*, 84: Oinomaus
	Poetic Astronomy, ii
ca. 160–176 CE	Pausanias *Description of Greece*, 5.1.3 - 7;
	5.13.1; 6.21.9; 8.14.10 - 11
170–245 CE	Philostratus *Imagines*, I.30: Pelops
ca. 200–245 CE	Philostratus the Younger *Imagines*, 9: Pelops
	First Vatican Mythographer, 22:
	Myrtilus; Atreus et Thyestes
	Second Vatican Mythographer, 146:
	Oinomaus

LINE 82: Pelops, in his plea to Poseidon, specifies that the gifts came from *Cyprian* Aphrodite, the manifestation of the goddess which ruled masculine loves.

LINE 91: Pindar, I.70-87, tr. from B. Sergent.

LAIUS AND GOLDENHORSE

410 BCE   Euripides *Chrysippus*, Fr. 840
140 BCE   Apollodorus *Library and Epitome*, 3.5.5
1st c. CE   Hyginus *Fables*, 85: Chrysippus; 243:
Women who Committed Suicide
ca. 160–176 CE   Pausanias *Description of Greece*, 6.20.7;
9.5.5-10
ca. 200 CE   Athenaeus *The Deipnosophists*, XIII: 602

LINE 17: The name of the boy is rendered here in translation, the only instance this technique is used in the current work, to underline its significance in the Pelops cycle. The theme of the Goldenhorse reappears throughout the three stories, and it is emphasized by the name of Pelops' wife: Hippodamia, which translates as Tamer of Horses.

LINE 101: Pelops was a central figure of Greek myth, though he is perhaps less known today than some of the other heroes. His influence, and the repercussions of his acts, touch many of the best-known figures of Greek myth. Here follows a brief epilogue to the House of Tantalus trilogy, setting out the main story line:

> King Pelops ruled wisely and with courage for many years over Pisa and Olympia, which he took from a neighboring king. He rests by the ford of the Alpheus, his tomb standing beside an altar thronged with visitors and splendid offerings. The people still sing his praises in Olympia every four years, for he is the patron hero of the greatest contest of them all, the Olympic games – they are nothing other than his memorial sacrifices. To this day his people honor him: all of western Greece, the land he conquered, bears the name he gave it: "Pelops' Island," Peloponnesus. But in his own time, his house was burdened with misfortune, the bitter price for killing Myrtilus.
>
> His twin sons, Atreus and Thyestes, paid dearly for their father's misdeed: An avalanche of destruction and deceit crushed them, crushed their children too. After Pelops cast them out,

they took refuge in Mycenae. There the people welcomed them with open arms, but Thyestes trampled on his luck, polluting his brother's house: for many years he lay in secret with Atreus' wife. Later, when the twins competed for the throne of Mycenae, Atreus outwitted his brother and ran him out of town. But when he found out about his wife's betrayal, victory stuck in his throat. He seized Thyestes' three children, cut their heads off, cooked their limbs. Then he invited his brother back for a feast, to renew their friendship, he said. He wined and dined him, then brought out the bloody heads, revealing to Thyestes that he had glutted himself on the flesh of his own murdered sons. Thyestes could not strike back in kind, for he feared some of Atreus' children might be his own. But he expressly fathered another son, Aegisthus, who avenged the deed many years later, plunging his father's sword right through Atreus' heart.

Still the gods were not appeased, and the curse stormed on. Atreus had a famous son, Agamemnon, who led the Greeks against the Trojans. While he was gone, his wife hardly pined for him, for he had murdered two of her children. She took his cousin, Thyestes' son Aegisthus, to her bed and flaunted him throughout the city. Agamemnon fought for ten years at Troy, and did not die in battle. Fate had other plans for him. Death found him inside his own house. He was murdered by his wife and her lover in his bath, on the day of his return. Only his son, Orestes, escaped the slaughter and hid in a distant land. When he came of age he returned to avenge his father, killed Aegisthus, killed his own mother, and in return the furies drove him mad.

DIFFERENT LOVES - PART II

1   The section detailing Lycinus' travels up to this point has been left out of this compilation.
2   Homer, *Odyssey*, Tr. R. Fagles, New York: Viking, 1996, VIII. 169
3   Ibid. XVII. 454
4   A play on *philo-neoi* (lovers of the young) and *philo-sophoi* (lovers of wisdom).
5   Euripides, *Phoenissae*, 529-530

ZEUS AND GANYMEDE

For this tale, the bulk of the references is included below, to better illustrate the process by which all the present stories were restored.

700 BCE   Homer *Iliad* 5.265ff; 20.215-235;
...*gave Tros full payment for stealing Ganymede*
...*strongest stallions under the dawn*
...*the most handsome of mortal men*
...*the gods snatched him away to bear the cup of Zeus and live among the immortals*

7th c. BCE   Anonymous *Homeric Hymn to Aphrodite* 202ff.
...*wise Zeus carried off golden-haired Ganymede because of his beauty, to be amongst the Deathless Ones and pour drink for the gods in the house of Zeus — a wonder to see — honored by all the immortals as he draws the red nectar from the golden bowl. But grief that could not be soothed filled the heart of Tros; for he knew not whither the heaven-sent whirlwind had caught up his dear son, so that he mourned him always, unceasingly, until Zeus pitied him and gave him high-stepping horses such as carry the immortals as recompense for his son. These he gave him as a gift. And at the command of Zeus, the Guide, the slayer of Argus, told him all, and how his son would be deathless and unageing, even as the gods. So when Tros heard these tidings from Zeus, he no longer kept mourning but rejoiced in his heart and rode joyfully with his storm-footed horses..*

b. 495 BCE – d. 406 BCE Sophocles, *The Colchian Women*
[after Athenaeus, 602]
...*Setting Zeus's majesty aflame with his thighs.*

410 BCE   Euripides *Iphigenia in Aulis* p. 47
Chorus: ...*There was Ganymede, the darling of Zeus' bed, drawing libations of wine from deep in the bowls of gold.*

250 BCE   Apollonios Rhodios *Argonautika* III. 115-126
[Episode in which Eros beats Ganymede at dice.]

140 BCE   Apollodorus *Library and Epitome*, iii.12.2
...*Ganymede, for the sake of his beauty, Zeus caught up on an eagle
and appointed him cupbearer of the gods in heaven...*

1st c. BCE   Diodorus Siculus *Histories* 4.75.3
*And Ganymedes, who excelled all men in beauty, was snatched up by
the gods to serve as the cupbearer of Zeus.*

19 BCE   Virgil *Aeneid* 5. 252 - 260
*There Ganymede is wrought with living art, Chasing thro' Ida's
groves the trembling hart: Breathless he seems, yet eager to pursue;
When from aloft descends, in open view, The bird of Jove, and, sous-
ing on his prey, With crooked talons bears the boy away. In vain, with
lifted hands and gazing eyes, His guards behold him soaring thro' the
skies, And dogs pursue his flight with imitated cries.*

1CE – 8 CE   Ovid *Metamorphoses* 10.155ff.
*The king of the gods was once afire with love for Phrygian
Ganymedes and hit upon a guise that, just this once, he thought might
be more suitable than being Jove himself: a bird. But of all birds, he
thought that one alone was worthiest; the bird with force enough to
carry Jove's own thunderbolts. Without delay Jove beat the air with his
deceiving wings, snatched up the Trojan boy. And even now, despite the
wrath of Juno, he still fulfills his role, the page of Jove, the boy pre-
pares Jove's nectar, fills his cups.*

2nd c. CE   Hyginus *Poetica Astronomica*
II.16 Eagle
*the eagle which is said to have snatched Ganymede up and given him
to his lover, Jove*
II.29 Aquarius, or Water Bearer
*Many have said he is Ganymede, whom Jupiter is said to have made
a cupbearer of the gods, snatching him up from his parents because of
his beauty. So he is shown as if pouring water from a jar.*

170 CE   Lucian *Dialogues of the Gods*
[Satire based on the Ganymede myth, featuring
Ganymede as a naive shepherd boy keen on getting back
to his flocks, playing with deceitful Eros, and Hera's fits
of jealousy.]

First Vatican Mythographer
184 Ganymede
*Ganymede, son of Tros, whose first beauty all the other Trojans were
fond of...*

Second Vatican Mythographer
198 Ganymede
*...because of the beauty of his body subjected himself to masculine pas-
sions in infamy. .*

PAGE 44: Tondo (central medallion) of kylix (wine cup used at sym-
posia) depicting Zeus laying hands on Ganymede, who holds a cock (a
traditional love gift) and reaches to catch the god's falling scepter.

LINE 96: The original myth predates Homeric times. Plato suggests (in
the *Laws)* the story came from Crete, which would be consistent with
the Cretan pederastic initiation rites recorded by Ephorus. These rites
paralleled closely key aspects of the Zeus and Ganymede story: The
boy underwent a ritual kidnapping, his family made a show of resistance, after which the boy was taken by his abductor to live in the
mountains for a set period, after which they rejoined the community
and the boy received ritual gifts marking the completion of the rite of
passage. These gifts, a bull, weapons, and a cup, symbolized his formal
entry into the adult world, and the three key aspects of the role he was
about to assume: agriculture, warfare, and religion.

Over time the myth changed. The eagle made its appearance, the
story became the stuff of comedy and farce (Aristophanes, in *The Peace,*
has his protagonist fly to Olympus on the back of a dung beetle fond
of well-kneaded manure), and stayed that way, from classical times to
the days of Lucian.

HERCULES AND HYLAS

7th c. BCE	Homer *Odyssey*, 12.072
350–310 BCE	Theocritus *Idylls*, 13
310–250 (?) BCE	Callimachus *Aetia (Causes)*, 24.
	Thiodamas the Dryopian *Fragments*, 160.
	Hymn to Artemis
c. 250 BCE	Apollonios Rhodios *Argonautika*, I. 1175 - 1280
140 BCE	Apollodorus *Library and Epitome* 1.9.19, 2.7.7
50–15 BCE	Sextus Propertius *Elegies*, i.20.17ff
8 CE–18 CE	Ovid *Ibis*, 488
1st c. CE	Gaius Valerius Flaccus *Argonautica*, I.110,
	III.535, 560, IV.1-57
1st c. CE	Hyginus *Fables*,14. Argonauts Assembled
170–245 CE	Philostratus the Elder *Images*, ii.24 Thiodamas
	First Vatican Mythographer, 49.
	Hercules et Hylas

LINE 3: Theocritus, Idyll 13. From *Idylls and Epigrams* (tr. D. Hine). Chicago: University of Chicago Press, 2000

LINE 48: Many of the details of Hercules' encounter with Thiodamas have been lost, but much can be inferred from surviving fragments of Callimachus and Philostratus, the present reconstruction being one possible version.

PAGE 56: The Ficoroni cist is an Etruscan bronze container for sacred objects, used in religious processions, signed by Novus Plautios, and made around 325 BCE. This image is part of an engraving encircling the barrel. The Ficoroni cist is replete with depictions of male love: Dionysus stands on the lid, flanked by two ithyphallic satyrs, and the cast bronze feet show Hercules and Iolaus (another of his beloveds) together with Eros. The engraving consists of a series of scenes depicting the Argonauts.

Some interpret the design as representing two separate events, one being the arrival of Polydeuces in Bebrycia (not visible in this view), and the other, the landing in Mysia. Hylas is identified by the hydria (water jug) at his feet and by his youth. His affectionate embrace identifies his lover, Hercules, wearing a helmet. The latter is shown without the club or lion pelt, his usual attributes. Though the image does not depict an event in the story as we know it (the two heroes seem to be getting ready for a contest, or perhaps a hunt), it is good to keep in mind that the details of the stories varied a great deal over time and from one place to another.

Others hold that the whole engraving depicts one single story, the conclusion of the fight between Polydeuces (Pollux) and Amycus, king of Bebrycia (here also the image diverges from known versions of the story, in which Amycus is killed outright rather than bound), in which case the lovers, though still Argonauts, must remain nameless.

[The identification of Hylas and Hercules is courtesy of Giovanni Dall'Orto.]

LINE 83: Hera's love for Jason is mentioned as far back as Homer, in Odyssey, 12.072. He claims she stopped the clashing rocks for him, though others attribute the feat to Orpheus. Her gift of fair wind is a modern invention, unlike the stiff breeze with which she chases the Argo off the Mysian shore.

ORPHEUS

462 BCE Pindar *Pythian Odes*, 4.176

c. 420 BCE Roman marble bas-relief, copy of a Greek original from the late 5th c.

c. 400 BCE Aristophanes, *The Frogs* 1032

3rd c. BCE Phanocles, *Erotes e Kaloi*, 15

c. 250 BCE Apollonios Rhodios, *Argonautika*, i.2

140 BCE Apollodorus *Library and Epitome* I.3.2

1st c. BCE Diodorus Siculus *Histories* I.23, I.96, III.65, IV.25

50–1 BCE Conon *Narrations*, 45

37–30 BCE Virgil *Georgics*, IV.456

23 BCE Horace *Odes*, I.12; *Ars Poetica* 391-407

8 CE Ovid *Metamorphoses* X.1-85, XI.1-65

5th c. CE Anonymous *Argonautiques Orphiques*

1st c. CE Seneca *Hercules Furens* 569

2nd c. CE Hyginus *Poetica Astronomica* II.7 Lyre

143–176 CE Pausanias *Description of Greece* 2.30.2, 9.30.4, 10.7.2

c. 400 CE Anonymous *The Clementine Homilies* Homily V Chapter XV.-Unnatural Lusts.

c. 450 CE Stobaeus *Anthologium* Second Vatican Mythographer, 44. *Orpheus*

LINE 1: Orpheus may or may not have been a historical personage. The ancients themselves were of two minds about him. They did agree that, real or not, he was already an ancient figure in Classical times. That he was primarily a priest of Dionysus, even an avatar of the god, is apparent from the parallels between his life and that of the wine god. They both traveled to Egypt, both descended to the Underworld to bring back a woman, and both were torn to pieces by enemies. Incidentally, Dionysus also resembles another, much later religious figure. He was a son of the God of Heaven, fathered on a virgin, appointed by his Father to be king over mankind, whom he came to liberate. Indeed one of his epithets was "Father Liber."

LINE 4: The connection between Dionysus, the god of wine, and Orpheus, the paramount prophet of male love is consistent with the association between mythical beloveds and magical or inebriating substances (Ganymede – nectar and the vine; Pelops – ambrosia; Narcissus – narcissus oil; and Dionysus himself, whose nature is the union of the vine and male love). The medieval Islamic construct of the wine boy as object of desire may be a late echo of this same complex.

LINE 84: The love between Orpheus and Calais seems to be a relatively late literary invention (the days of Alexander the Great), as opposed to his relationship with Apollo and his teachings to the Thracians, which appear grounded in ancient myth.

DIFFERENT LOVES - PART III

1   Iliad, I.152
2   Iliad, VIII.15
3   The time (according to Varro) between the Ogygian deluge and the first Olympiad. This was the age termed "fabulous" by the Greeks, for it was the age of myth, the time of the heroic deeds, and of the first great poets (Orpheus, Homer, Hesiod, etc.), the time before it could be said to have been "the time before time." (Sir Thomas Browne, *Pseudodoxia Epidemica* VI:vi)
4   Hesiod *Works and Days*, 318, 11, 12, 13
5   Euripides *Hippolytus*, 618
6   The love of Cybele for Attis, which resulted in his death.
7   Menander, Fr. 718
8   School for athletics and martial arts
9   Euripides *Iphigenia in Tauris*, 311-312
10 Ibid. 598-599 and 603-605
11 Callimachus *Aetia* Fr. 41
12 Xenophon *Symposium* VIII, *The Lacedemonian Republic*, II
13 Callimachus, Fr. 571
14 In this Roman empire fountain mosaic depicting the end of the Erymanthian boar hunt, the boy beside Hercules is probably Iolaus, his helper in that exploit as well as others. In ancient times the two were widely assumed to have been intimate. As Plutarch tells us: "And as to the [male] loves of Hercules, it is difficult to record them because of their number; but those who think that Iolaus was one of them do to this day worship and honor him, and make their loved ones swear their faith at his tomb." And also, "It is a tradition likewise that Iolaus, who assisted Hercules in his labors and fought at his side, was beloved of him; and Aristotle observes that even in his time lovers pledged their faith at Iolaus' tomb." [Plutarch *Eroticus*, par. 17, *Life of Pelopidas*]

His age, said to have been about sixteen at the time of Hercules' labors, itself points to such a relationship, and his role as Hercules' charioteer is also suggestive of male love. The association between the roles of chariot driver and beloved can be seen in the stories of Pelops and Poseidon, and Laius and Chrysippus,

as well as in the historical battalion known as the Sacred Band of
Thebes, one hundred and fifty pairs of lovers, each consisting of a
fighter and his charioteer. They remained invincible until their last
battle, against Philip II, father of Alexander the Great, in which
they died to the last man. Philip himself fell prey shortly after-
wards to one of his beloveds: he was assassinated by a jealous
boyfriend.

APOLLO AND HYACINTHUS

c. 700 BCE	Homer *Illiad*, ii.595 - 600
5th c. BCE	Various vase paintings
330 BCE	Palaephatus *On Unbelievable Tales*, 46. Hyacinthus
140 BCE	Apollodorus *Library* I.3.3
1–8 CE	Ovid *Metamorphoses* 10. 162-219
160–176 CE	Pausanias *Description of Greece*, 3.1.3, 3.19.4
170–245 CE	Philostratus the Elder *Images*, i.24 Hyacinthus Philostratus the Younger *Images*, 14. Hyacinthus
170 CE	Lucian *Dialogues of the Gods*, 14 First Vatican Mythographer,197. Thamyris et Musae

LINE 117: This festival was one of the principal Spartan festivals. It
lasted three full days, and was open to slaves and foreigners as well. The
first day and a half the feasting was held in mourning for the death of
Hyacinthus, and the second half of the festival was a celebration of his
rebirth, a part of the story we no longer have. The story itself can be
understood as an archetypal Greek and Indo-European rite of passage,
in which the protagonist, after a period of pederastic initiation, dies as
an adolescent and is reborn as an adult. B. Sergent, cf., pp.81-96

NARCISSUS

8 CE Ovid *Metamorphoses* III. 340–350, 415–510
143–176 CE Pausanias *Description of Greece,* 9.31.7

LINE 1: This story is part of a constellation of legends associating beautiful youths with inebriating substances. Ganymede of course is associated with nectar, and with wine, as symbolized by the gift of the golden vine, as is Pelops, who poured nectar for Poseidon. Ampelos is the spirit of the vine, and Narcissus is linked with narcissus oil, another intoxicating substance.

LINE 59: Monologue is informed by Allen Mandelbaum's translation of Ovid.

LINE 84: Significantly, "narcissus" and "narcotic" are cognates sharing the same Greek root, "narke" meaning "numbness, deadness."

ACHILLES AND PATROCLUS

700 BCE   Homer *Iliad* 9.308, 16.2, 11.780, 23.54,
476 BCE   Pindar *Olympian Ode* IX
495 BCE   Aeschylus *Myrmidons* F135-36
405 BCE   Euripides *Iphigenia in Aulis*
388–367 BCE   Plato *Symposium*, 179e
96 CE   Statius *Achilleid* 161, 174, 182

LINE 92: The issue of the relative ages of the two heroes has been a bone of contention since Classical times. Homer clearly asserted that Achilles was the younger of the two (Iliad, 11.787) but at the same time asserted he was dominant in the relationship, making mincemeat of traditional lover/beloved roles. Nonetheless they were widely assumed to have been lovers, as evidenced, for example, by an account by Arrian (1.12.1) in which Alexander the Great and his beloved Hephaiston, on their way to war, stop to sacrifice at the twin tombs of the heroes, Alexander to Achilles and Hephaiston to Patroclus.

LINE 119: From a fragment of The Myrmidons, a lost play by Aeschylus. [The fact that none of the plays with male love as a topic have survived bears mention here.]

LINE 125: Though it is universally accepted that Homer did not make mention of male love, reputedly an unfit topic for myth, it is hard to see what other intention can reasonably be imputed to Thetis' comment (Iliad, 24.130), especially as understood by an audience steeped in the practice. In the Odyssey, likewise, there are suggestive allusions in the relationship between Telemachus and Pisistratus, though coevals according to Homer.

DIFFERENT LOVES - PART IV

1   A buskin is a thick-soled shoe that can be worn on either foot.
2   Legendary fools. See Aristophanes, *Frogs* 991 and Lucian, *The Lover of Lies* 3
3   Euripides *Orestes*, 14.
4   Unknown
5   Homer *Iliad*, Tr. R. Fagles, New York: Viking, 1990, IX, 191
6   Aeschylus *The Myrmidons*, Fr. 136
7   "Komastes," participants at certain feasts of Dionysus.
8   The legendary place where the hero met his end on a pyre.

AFTERWORD

1   Allan Bloom, Tr., New York: Basic Books, 1991
2   Bernard Evslin, *Heroes, Gods and Monsters of the Greek Myths*, New York: Four Winds Press, 1967

STORYTELLER'S POSTSCRIPT

1   A good example of such omissions occurs in the Greek myth of creation itself. We are told (by Edith Hamilton) that Cronus, goaded by his mother, Gea, strikes Uranus, his father, and "wounds him terribly." And she tells us that Aphrodite (Venus), the goddess of desire, is born from the foam of the sea. The ancient version is quite different, powerfully so. Cronus, armed with a sickle, waits in ambush and strikes off his father's genitals, which he then hurls down into the Ocean, the river encircling the Earth. The tossing waves of the sea churn the spilled seed of the father god into a foam, which spontaneously gives rise to the goddess of love.

2   Sappho, the poet from the island of Lesbos, which gave female love its current name, charmed generation after generation of readers for fifteen hundred years with her sweet poems of desire. She was regarded as the most talented of all women poets, as accomplished as any man, if not more so. Her works survived until about a thousand years ago, when Pope Gregory VII (in office 1073-1085) had all known copies of her books gathered and burned.*
*Rictor Norton, *The Myth of the Modern Homosexual*, London: Cassell, 1997

3   See Lucian's *Different Loves*, Part II, in this volume.

Illustration Sources

COVER

The Greek vase painting on the front and back covers is taken from a 5th c. BCE Attic column krater titled "Orpheus and the Thracians" in the collection of the State Museum of Berlin. The object is reproduced *in toto* on page 65.

BELOVED CHARIOTEERS

PAGE X: Quadriga and Charioteer; Black-figure oinochoe, Athens 550–530 BCE. Amasis painter. B524 © The British Museum, London

PAGE 2: Courtship Ritual; Amphora, 5th c. BCE. Painter of Cambridge, SH 1468 WAF. Courtesy of the Staatliche Antikensammlungen und Glyptothek, Munich

PAGE 5: Ganymede and Eagle, view A; Antonine period copy of late 4th c. BCE. Greek original. 6355. Museo Archeologico Nazionale, Naples. Photo © A. Calimach

PAGE 6: Hercules, Eros, and Iolaus; Ficoroni cist foot, Bronze casting, late 4th c. BCE, Novus Plautios, Museo Etrusco di Villa Giulia, Rome. Photo © A. Calimach

DIFFERENT LOVES – PART I

PAGE 9: Plato's School, Mosaic, Pompeii, 1st c. BCE. 124.545. Museo Archeologico Nazionale, Naples. Courtesy of the Soprintendenza Archeologica delle Province di Napoli e Caserta.

PAGE 10: Seduction Scenes (Side B) Man with Youth and Love Gift, Athenian black figure amphora, 550–530 BCE. Painter of Amasis, F26. Louvre, Paris © Photo Réunion des Musées Nationaux / Art Resource, NY

TANTALUS AND THE OLYMPIANS

PAGE 13: Zeus, Bronze, 909 © The British Museum, London

PAGE 14: Poseidon with Trident Chasing Pelops (side A: Poseidon), Attic red figure column krater, AS IV 3737. Courtesy, Kunsthistorisches Museum, Vienna

PAGE 15: Poseidon with Trident Chasing Pelops (side B: Fleeing youth), Attic red figure column krater, AS IV 3737. Courtesy, Kunsthistorisches Museum, Vienna

PAGE 17: Tantalus, Intaglio gem ring, 618 © The British Museum, London

PELOPS IN PISA

PAGE 18: Pisatan Scenes (Side A) Hippodamia and Sterope, Apulian amphora, Ruvo, Varnese painter, F331 © The British Museum, London

PAGE 21: Poseidon and Pelops, Attic red figure hydria, 400-375 BCE. 21.88.162. The Metropolitan Museum of Art, Rogers Fund, 1921. Photograph © 1986 The Metropolitan Museum of Art, New York

PAGE 22: Helios in Flying Quadriga, Red-figure calyx krater, Athens, 430 BCE. Blacas coll. E466 © The British Museum, London

PAGE 23: Pisatan Scenes (Side B, detail) Oinomaus, Apulian amphora, Ruvo, Varnese painter, F331 © The British Museum, London

PAGES 24–25: Pelops and Hippodameia Racing; Photo © Maicar Förlag - GML, www.hsa.brown.edu/~maicar

PAGE 26: Oinomaus and Myrtilus, Apulian volute krater, detail, 3256. Museo Archeologico Nazionale, Naples. Courtesy, Soprintendenza Archeologica delle Province di Napoli e Caserta.

PAGE 29: Pelops and Myrtilus, Apulian calyx krater, Ruvo, 350–340 BCE. Lycurgus painter, F271 © The British Museum, London

LAIUS AND GOLDENHORSE

PAGE 30: Boy and Horse, Marble relief, Villa of Hadrian, Tivoli, 125 CE. Greek sculpture, 2206 © The British Museum, London

PAGE 33: Laius Abducting Chrysippus, detail, Apulian red-figure volute krater, ca. 320 BCE, White Saccos Painter, 77.AE.14. The J. Paul Getty Museum, Malibu, California. Gift of Gordon McLendon

PAGE 34: Hippodamia, detail, Apulian calyx krater, Ruvo, 350–340 BCE. Lycurgus painter, F271 © The British Museum, London.

DIFFERENT LOVES – PART II

PAGE 36: Capitoline Venus, Marble, 200–150 BCE, Ma 335. Louvre, Paris © Photo Réunion des Musées Nationaux – Hervé Lewandowski / Art Resource, NY

PAGE 39: Zeus and Ganymede, Attic red figure pelike, 1416 Courtesy, National Archaeological Museum, Athens

PAGE 41: Symposium, Girl Dancing, Kylix tondo, Vulci, Bassegio collection, 490–480 BCE. Byrgos painter, E68 © The British Museum, London

ZEUS AND GANYMEDE

PAGE 44: Zeus Courting Ganymede, symposium cup (kylix), 5th c. BCE, Penthesileia Painter, 9351. Courtesy of the Museo Archeologico Nazionale, Ferrara.

PAGE 46: Zeus, Red figure krater, 500–490 BCE, Painter of Berlin, G 175 (side B). Louvre, Paris © Photo Réunion des Musées Nationaux – Hervé Lewandowski /Art Resource, NY

PAGE 47: Ganymede, Red figure krater, 500–490 BCE, Painter of Berlin, G 175 (side A). Louvre, Paris © Photo Réunion des Musées Nationaux – Hervé Lewandowski /Art Resource, NY

PAGE 50: Ganymede and Eagle, view B; Antonine period copy of late 4th c. BCE. Greek original. 6355. Museo Archeologico Nazionale, Naples. Photo © A. Calimach

HERCULES AND HYLAS

PAGE 53: Hercules and Telephus; 1st–2nd c. CE Roman copy of a Greek original, MA75. Louvre, Paris © Photo Réunion des Musées Nationaux / Art Resource, NY

PAGE 54: Hercules Slaying an Ox; Attic black figure lekythos, AS IV 86. Courtesy, Kunsthistorisches Museum, Vienna

PAGE 56: Hercules and Hylas; Ficoroni cist, Bronze engraving, late 4th c. BCE, Novus Plautios, Museo Etrusco di Villa Giulia, Rome. Courtesy, Soprintendenza Archeologica per l'Etruria Meridionale

PAGE 59: The Abduction of Hylas; Marble wall panel in opus sectile, 1st half of the 4th c. CE. Museo Nazionale Romano Palazzo Massimo Alle Terme, Rome. Courtesy, Soprintendenza Archeologica di Roma

PAGE 61: Hercules with the Hesperidean Apples, Marble, Museo Archeologico Nazionale, Naples. Photo © A. Calimach

ORPHEUS

PAGE 62: Child Dionysus and Satyr, Roman copy after Greek original, Museo Archeologico Nazionale, Naples. Photo © A. Calimach

PAGE 65: Orpheus and Thracians; column krater, 5th c. V.I.3172. Antikensammlung, Staatliche Museen zu Berlin - Preussischer Kulturbesitz

PAGE 66: Maenad and Satyrs in Bacchic Procession; Marble, Rome, 100 CE from 4th c. BCE Greek sculpture, 2193 © The British Museum, London

PAGE 68: Kithara Player; Attic red figure amphora, 490 BCE. Berlin Painter 56.171.38. The Metropolitan Museum of Art, Fletcher Fund, 1956. Photograph © 1998 The Metropolitan Museum of Art, New York

PAGE 71: Orpheus, Eurydice and Hermes; Marble. Ma 588. Louvre, Paris © Photo Réunion des Musées Nationaux – Hervé Lewandowski / Art Resource, NY

PAGE 72: The Death of Orpheus; Red figure amphora, c. 445–430 BCE, Painter of Philae, G 436. Louvre, Paris © Photo Réunion des Musées Nationaux – Hervé Lewandowski / Art Resource, NY

PAGE 73: Dionysus with Satyrs; Ficoroni cist lid, Bronze casting, late 4th c. BCE, Novus Plautios, Museo Etrusco di Villa Giulia, Rome. Photo © A. Calimach

DIFFERENT LOVES – PART III

PAGE 74: Eros; Marble, Museo Archeologico Nazionale, Naples. Photo © A. Calimach

PAGE 79: Symposium Scene, Kylix tondo, Vulci, 490–480 BCE, Painter of Paris gigantomachy, E70 © The British Museum, London

PAGE 82: Music Lesson, Athenian red-figure kylix, tondo, 460-450 BCE. Eumaion painter. G467 Louvre, Paris. Photo © A. Calimach

PAGE 85: Hercules and Iolaus; Fountain Mosaic from the Anzio Nymphaeum, detail, 1st c. CE. Museo Nazionale Romano Palazzo Massimo Alle Terme, Rome. Photo © A. Calimach

APOLLO AND HYACINTHUS

PAGE 86: Apollo and Artemis; Attic red figure hydria, detail AS IV 3739. Courtesy, Kunsthistorisches Museum, Vienna

PAGE 88: Zephyrus and Hyacinthus, Kylix, 490–485 BCE, Douris. 9531. Courtesy, Museum of Fine Arts, Boston. Reproduced with permission. © 2000 Museum of Fine Arts, Boston. All rights reserved.

PAGE 89: Blinding of Thamyris, Attic red figure hydria, G291. Courtesy, Ashmolean Museum, Oxford

PAGE 90: Hyacinthus on the Flying Swan, Attic red figure skyphos, AS IV 191. Courtesy, Kunsthistorisches Museum, Vienna

PAGE 93: Discobolus, Bronze, restored from fragmentary copies of an original by Myron, from the middle of the 5th c. BCE. Museo Nazionale Romano, Photo Coll. Paribeni

NARCISSUS

PAGE 94: Narcissus, Louvre, Paris. Photo © A. Calimach

PAGE 97: Nemesis. Marble, Roman. Ma 4873. Louvre, Paris © Photo Réunion des Musées Nationaux – Hervé Lewandowski /Art Resource, NY

PAGE 99: Narcissus, Echo and Eros, Fresco (detail), Pompeii, 1st c. CE, 9380. Museo Archeologico Nazionale, Naples. Courtesy of the Soprintendenza Archeologica delle Province di Napoli e Caserta.

ACHILLES AND PATROCLUS

PAGE 100: Achilles Bandaging Patroclus, Kylix, 5th c. F2278. Antikensammlung, Staatliche Museen zu Berlin - Preussischer Kulturbesitz

PAGE 103: Achilles and Briseis, Red figure kylix, border, Athens, 480 BCE. Briseis painter, E76. © The British Museum, London

PAGE 104: Achilles and Cheiron, Fresco. Museo Archeologico Nazionale, Naples. Courtesy, Soprintendenza Archeologica delle Province di Napoli e Caserta.

PAGE 107: Thetis, Attic red figure kylix, AS IV 96. Courtesy, Kunsthistorisches Museum, Vienna

DIFFERENT LOVES – PART IV

PAGE 110: Pan and Daphnis, 2nd c. BCE Roman copy of a Greek original, 6329. Museo Archeologico Nazionale, Naples. Photo © A. Calimach

PAGE 113: Sleeping Eros, Bronze, Rhodos, 3rd–2nd c. BCE, 43.11.4. The Metropolitan Museum of Art, Rogers Fund, 1943. Photograph © 1985 The Metropolitan Museum of Art, New York

AFTERWORD

PAGE 114: Venus of Arles; Marble after Praxiteles. c. 360 BCE. Louvre, Paris © Photo Réunion des Musées Nationaux / Art Resource, NY

STORYTELLER'S POSTSCRIPT

PAGE 118: Head of Aphrodite /Anahita; Bronze, Armenia Minor, 200–100 BCE. 266 © The British Museum, London

BIBLIOGRAPHY

PAGE 161: Hermes resting, Bronze, copy of 4th c. BCE. Greek original from school of Lyssipos, 5625. Museo Archeologico Nazionale, Naples. Courtesy, Soprintendenza Archeologica delle Province di Napoli e Caserta.

PAGE 164: New Arms for Achilles, Red figure pelike, Athens 470 BCE. E363 © The British Museum, London

INDEXED GLOSSARY

PAGE 178: Seduction Scenes (Side A) Winged Divinity, Hoplite, and Ephebe; Athenian black figure amphora, 550–530 BCE. Painter of Amasis. Louvre, Paris © Photo Réunion des Musées Nationaux /Art Resource, NY

Bibliography

Aeschylus. *Fragments, The Myrmidons*: 228, 229 (ed. Mette),
(after K. J. Dover, *Greek Homosexuality*, New York: Vintage, 1980).

Anonymous. *Argonautiques Orphiques*, (tr. Francis Vian).
Paris: Les Belles Lettres, 1987.

———. *Homeric Hymn to Aphrodite*, (tr. Hugh G. Evelyn-White).
Cambridge: Loeb Classical Library, Harvard University Press,
1988.

———. *The Clementine Homilies*, Homily V Chapter XV. Unnatural
Lusts, Christian Classics Ethereal Library, Calvin College, 2001.
www.ccel.org/fathers2/ANF-08/anf08-49.htm#P4047_1215482

Apollodorus. *Library and Epitome*, (ed. Sir James George Frazer).
Perseus Digital Library, Tufts University, 2001.
www.perseus.tufts.edu

Apollonios Rhodios. *The Argonautika*, (tr. Peter Green). Berkeley:
University of California Press, 1997.

Aristophanes. *Peace*, (after K. J. Dover, *Greek Homosexuality*
New York: Vintage, 1980).

Athenaeus, *The Deipnosophists*, (tr.Charles Burton Gulick). Cambridge:
Loeb Classical Library, Harvard University Press, 1937.

Bagemihl, Bruce. *Biological Exuberance: Animal Homosexuality and Natural
Diversity*, New York: St. Martin's Press, 1999.

Bode, G.H., ed., *Scriptores Rerum Mythicarum Latini*, (First Vatican Mythographer *Ganymede, Hercules et Hylas, Thamyris et Musae;* Second Vatican Mythographer 44 *Orpheus*, 198 *Ganymede*). Celle: 1834.

Callimachus. *Aetia, Iambi, Hecale and Other Fragments*, (tr.C. A. Trypanis). Cambridge: Loeb Classical Library, Harvard University Press, 1958.

Clement of Alexandria. *Exhortation to the Greeks*, (tr. G. W. Butterworth). Cambridge: Loeb Classical Library, Harvard University Press, 1919.

Conon. *Narrations* 45, in W. K. C. Guthrie, *Orpheus and Greek Religion*, London: Methuen, 1952.

Diodorus Siculus. *Histories*, Cambridge: Loeb Classical Library, Harvard University Press, 1992.

Euripides. *Chryssipus* Fr. 840 (after K. J. Dover, *Greek Homosexuality* New York: Vintage, 1980.)

———. *Hippolytus*, (tr. E. P. Coleridge). Internet Classics Archive, 2000. classics.mit.edu/Browse/browse-Euripides.html

———. *Iphigenia in Aulis*, (tr. Nicholas Rudall). Chicago: Ivan R. Dee, 1997.

———. *Iphigenia in Tauris*, (tr. Robert Potter) Internet Classics Archive, 2000. classics.mit.edu/Browse/browse-Euripides.html

———. *Orestes*, (tr. John Peck and Frank Nisetich). New York: Oxford University Press, 1995.

———. *Phoenissae*, (tr. E. P. Coleridge). Internet Classics Archive, 2000. classics.mit.edu/Browse/browse-Euripides.html

———. *Rhesus*, Internet Classics Archive, 2000. classics.mit.edu/Browse/browse-Euripides.html

Graves, Robert. *The Greek Myths*, London: Penguin, 1955

Hesiod, *Works and Days* (tr. Hugh G. Evelyn-White).å Perseus Digital Library, Tufts University, 2001.å www.perseus.tufts.edu

Hermes resting

Homer. *The Iliad,* (tr. Robert Fagles). New York: Viking, 1990.

———. *The Odyssey,* (tr. Robert Fagles). New York: Viking, 1996.

Horace. *Odes* I.12, (ed. John Conington). Perseus Digital Library, Tufts University, 2001. www.perseus.tufts.edu

———. *Ars Poetica* 391-407 (tr. Leon Golden). Perseus Digital Library, Tufts University, 2001. www.perseus.tufts.edu

Hyginus. *Fables & Poetic Astronomy in The Myths of Hyginus* (tr. Mary Grant). Lawrence: Humanistic Studies No. 34, University of Kansas Publications, 1960.

Kerényi, C. *The Heroes of the Greeks,* (tr. H. J. Rose). New York: Grove Press, 1960.

Lucian of Samosate. *Erotes,* (Tr. as *Affairs of the Heart* by M.D. Macleod). Cambridge: Loeb Classical Library, Harvard University Press, 1967. (Tr. as *Les Amours* by Roger Peyrefitte). Paris: Flammarion, 1973.

———. *Dialogues of the Gods,* (tr. M.D. Macleod). Cambridge: Loeb Classical Library, Harvard University Press, 1961.

Norton, Rictor. *The Myth of the Modern Homosexual,* London: Cassell, 1997.

Ovid. *Metamorphoses,* (tr. Allen Mandelbaum). New York: Harcourt, Brace, 1993.

———. *Metamorphoses,* (ed. Brookes More). Perseus Digital Library, Tufts University, 2001, www.perseus.tufts.edu

Palaephatus. *On Unbelievable Tales,* (tr. Jacob Stern). Wauconda: Bolchazy-Carducci, 1996.

Pausanias. *Description of Greece,* (tr. W.H.S. Jones, and H.A. Ormerod). Perseus Digital Library, Tufts University, 2001. www.perseus.tufts.edu

Peyrefitte, Roger. *La Muse Garçonniere,* Paris: Flammarion, 1973

Phanocles. *Erotes e Kaloi,* (tr. Katherina Alexander) Amsterdam: Adolf M. Hakkert, 1988.

Philostratus the Elder. *Images*, (tr. Arthur Fairbanks). Cambridge: Loeb Classical Library, Harvard University Press, 1992.

Philostratus the Younger. *Images*, (tr. Arthur Fairbanks). Cambridge: Loeb Classical Library, Harvard University Press, 1992.

Pindar. *Olympian Odes*, Perseus Digital Library, Tufts University, 2001. www.perseus.tufts.edu

————. *Pythian Odes*, Perseus Digital Library, Tufts University, 2001. www.perseus.tufts.edu

Plato. *Symposium*, (tr. Tom Griffith). Berkeley: University of California Press, 1986.

Propertius, Sextus. *Elegies*, (ed. Vincent Katz). Perseus Digital Library, Tufts University, 2001. www.perseus.tufts.edu

Seneca. *Hercules Furens*, (tr. Frank J. Miller). Cambridge: Loeb Classical Library, Harvard University Press, 1988.

Sergent, Bernard, *Homosexuality in Greek Myth*, (tr. A. Goldhammer). Boston: Beacon Press, 1986.

Statius, Publius Papinius. *Achilleid*, (tr. J. H. Mozeley). Cambridge: Loeb Classical Library, Harvard University Press, 1992.

Theocritus. in *Greek Bucolic Poets*, (tr. J. M. Edmonds). Cambridge: Loeb Classical Library, Harvard University Press, 1912

————. *Idylls and Epigrams*, (tr. D. Hine). Chicago: University of Chicago Press, 2000

Valerius Flaccus, Gaius. *Argonautica*, (tr. J. H. Mozley). Cambridge: Loeb Classical Library, Harvard University Press, 1963

Virgil, *Aeneid*, (tr. John Dryden). Perseus Digital Library, Tufts University, 2001, www.perseus.tufts.edu

————. *Georgics*, (tr. J. B. Greenough). Perseus Digital Library, Tufts University, 2001, www.perseus.tufts.edu

New arms for Achilles

Indexed Glossary

Apollo: god of arts, divination, plagues, and healing;
lover of Orpheus and Hyacinthus.   4, 57, 63, 70, 83, *86-92*,
102, 106, 108, 117, 129, 140, 142, 154

Aquarius: constellation; youth bearing a water jar,
said to be Ganymede.   51, 135

Aquila: constellation; eagle with outspread wings,
above Aquarius; said to be Zeus' bird.

Areopagos: hill in Athens where the Athenian Council
(the Supreme Court) met.

Argo: the ship of the Argonauts.   57, 67, 71, 138

Argonauts: heroes, usually about 50 in number; members of
the expedition to retrieve the Golden Fleece.   67, 137, 138, 165

Argynnus: hero, beloved of Agamemnon.   126

Aristides the Milesian: writer of erotic stories, now lost;
lived in the 2nd c. BCE.   8

Aristophanes: Athenian comic poet and playwright,
445–386 BCE.   136, 139, 145, 159

Artemis: goddess of the hunt; sister of Apollo and
avenger of Ameinias.   96, 136, 154

Aspasia: patron of the arts and wife of Pericles,
accused of atheism by enemies, 5th c. BCE.   75

Athens: city-state, culturally and militarily dominant during
much of the Classical period.   40, 111, 147, 149, 150, 156, 157

Atreus: hero; son of Pelops, brother of Thyestes,
father of Agamemnon, ruler of Mycenae.   31, 34, 130-132

Bebrycia: barbarian land in northern Asia Minor,
visited by the Argonauts.   137, 138

Boreas: the god of the north wind; the spurned
lover of Hyacinthus in late versions of the story.

Hylas: hero; son of Thiodamas, beloved of
Hercules, taken by the river nymphs.   45, 47, 52, 55, *56*, 57, 58,
59, 60, 125, 126, 137, 138, 152, 159

Ida: mountain in Phrygia, close to Troy,
from which Zeus abducted Ganymede.   45, 47, 135

Iolaus: hero; Hercules' helper, nephew, and beloved.
Lovers and beloveds swore loyalty at his tomb.   2, 6, 7, 8, *85*,
126, 137, 141, 147, 154

Jason: hero; leader of the Argonauts and
Hera's protegee.   57, 60, 61, 138

King of the Gods, also **King of Heaven:** *see* Zeus.   4, 45, 46

Laius: hero; tutor and raper of Chrysippus
(Goldenhorse); murdered by his own son, Oedipus.   31, 32, *33*,
34, 35, 117, 131, 141, 150

Lemnian women: heroines; cursed with a
foul stench for not honoring Aphrodite.   8

Lernean swamp: notorious marsh; home of the
Hydra, and Dionysus' gate into the underworld.

Lernean heads: the Hydra's; if one was cut,
two grew back unless the stump was cauterized.   8

Lesbos: island in the northern Aegean,
directly east of Thrace.   73, 75, 146

Liriope: water nymph, mother of Narcissus; "Lilly Face."

Lord of the Sea: *see* Poseidon

Love: *see* Aphrodite

Lucian of Samosata: satirist, author (?) of
Erotes, (Different Loves); 120–190 CE.   127

Lyceum: gymnasium where philosophy was taught,
near ancient Athens.

Orpheus: mythic/historical prophet of Dionysus;
Apollo's pupil and beloved; first teacher of male love.   4, 63, 64,
65, 66, 67, 68, 69, 70, 71, 72, 73, 117,
138–141, 147, 153, 159, 160

Ovid: Roman poet, documented myths of male love
in *Metamorphoses*; 43 BCE–17 CE   2, 129, 135, 137,
139, 142, 143, 160

Paris: hero; son of Priam, abductor of Helen,
brother of Hector and lover of Antheus.   101, 108, 126

Patroclus: hero; son of Menoetius,
lover/beloved of Achilles.   IV, *100*, 101-109,
113, 117, 126, 144, 156

Peloponnese: peninsula making up all of
southern Greece, named after Pelops.

Pelops: hero, son of Tantalus, beloved of Poseidon;
king of Sipylus, then Pisa and Olympia.   4, 12, 14, *15*, 16, 17,
19, 20, *21*, *23*, *24*, 26-29, 31, 32, 34, 35,
124, 129, 130, 131, 140, 141, 143, 148, 149

Pericles: Athenian statesman and democrat;
defended Aspasia before a jury of 1500; 495–429 BCE.   43, 75

Phaedrus: Athenian citizen, after whom one of
Plato's dialogues was named, late 5th c. BCE.   40, 75, 76

Phocis: land north of Corinth, home of the Delphic oracle.   83

Phrygia: land in north-western Anatolia, home of Ganymede.   81

Pindar: elegiac poet, 518–438 BCE.   129, 130, 138, 144, 163

Pisa: town in the Peloponnese, seat of
Oinomaus and then of Pelops.   19-21, 24, 26, 27, 28, 31, 33,
130, 131, 149

Plato: Athenian philosopher, student of Socrates;
favored male love in his early works. 427–347 BCE.
IV, 2, 3, 9, 40, 116, 117, 123, 136, 144, 148, 163

Seduction scene

LOVERS' LEGENDS
THE GAY GREEK MYTHS

COMPOSED IN
MONOTYPE CENTAUR AND ADOBE LITHOS

HAIDUK PRESS LOGO
LINOTYPE BY RAYMOND VERDAGUER
HOMEPAGE.MAC.COM/RAYMONDSV

MAP ART BY JEFF GRYGNY
GRYGNY@XSITE.COM

DESIGNED AT
SEALEVEL, HALIFAX, NOVA SCOTIA
WWW.SEALEVEL.NS.CA

PRINTED, SMYTH-SEWN AND BOUND BY
SHERIDAN BOOKS
WWW.SHERIDANBOOKS.COM

HAIDUK PRESS
WWW.HAIDUKPRESS.COM